MIND YOUR BUSINESS LADY™

The Women Entrepreneurs Complete Guide To Doing What You Love & Getting Paid To Do It!

C. WOODS

> This book is intended for use as a stand-alone reference or in conjunction with the "Mind Your Business Lady" Course. The online Workbook referred to throughout this book is only available for those who also enroll in the course.
>
> TO ENROLL IN THE NEXT "MIND YOUR BUSINESS LADY" COURSE, PLEASE VISIT WWW.MINDYOURBUSINESSLADY.COM/COURSE TO REGISTER. ENTER DISCOUNT CODE "BOOK101" FOR A 10% DISCOUNT.

This book is designed to provide accurate and authoritative information in regard to the subject matter covered as of date of publication. It is understood that with the sale of this book, the author/publisher is not engaged in providing legal, accounting or other professional service. If legal advice, counsel or other professional service is required, the services of a professional in those fields should be sought.

"Mind Your Business Lady™" is a trademark of C. Woods, Oakland, California

©2020 C. Woods

All rights reserved.

Printed in the United States of America.

This publication may not be reproduced, stored in a retrieval system, transmitted in whole or in part, in any form or by any means, electronic, mechanical, photocopying, recorded, or otherwise, without the sole written permission of the Author. Any and all violations are illegal and punishable by law. The Author appreciates your purchasing and support of her rights.

To my clients,
This one is for you!

To my family & supporters,
You are the best!

TABLE OF CONTENTS

Foreword 1

CHAPTER 1:

THE STRUGGLE IS REAL 3

CHAPTER 2:

PURPOSE, PASSION, PROFIT 17

CHAPTER 3:

"MIND" YOUR BUSINESS LADY, IT PAYS 33

CHAPTER 4:

LEGALLY SPEAKING DOT THE I'S CROSS THE T'S 55

CHAPTER 5:

ONLINE VS. OFFLINE 73

CHAPTER 6:

ATTRACTING THE CLIENT OF YOUR DREAMS 87

CHAPTER 7:

READY, SET, LAUNCH SEQUENCE 105

CHAPTER 8:

BLAH TO BOOMING – BOOST YOUR BRAND 121

CHAPTER 9:

BIZ ON A BUDGET/MULTIPLE INCOME STREAMS 131

*BONUS #1:

W.I.N. STRATEGY TO SUCCESS 144

*BONUS #2:

YOUR CUSTOM BIZ ACTION PLAN 149

*BONUS #3:

SURPRISE, SURPRISE – SECRET GIFT FOR YOU! 153

INDEX 155

FOREWORD

Mind Your Business Lady is more than a book, it's a movement, it's a community of empowered Women Entrepreneurs learning how to do what she loves and get paid to do it. I am the "Mind Your Business Lady" in the flesh. It is my purpose, it is my passion to help as many purpose driven Women Entrepreneurs as God sends my way, learn how to use her God given gifts and talents to create wealth while serving others.

As women in business, we wear so many hats and I am not the exception. I am CEO of multiple businesses and CEO of my life. Like many of you readers, I am a wife, mom, daughter and grandmother, sister, aunt, niece, cousin and friend to many who count on me for so many things. So I know what it's like to be pulled in so many directions and wear the Super Woman cape 24/7. I often joke with clients and members of my Sistars Women's Empowerment Network that "You have to take the cape off sometime Sis!" Lol.

I wrote this book as a guide, a reference and to clear a path for all Women Entrepreneurs starting or growing her own business. Too often we get lost in the sauce and get stuck as we try our hardest to turn our vision and dreams to reality. No more Sis! No more guessing what to do and how to do it. No more trying to re-invent the wheel and figure everything out on your own. Time out for wasting money and time. Time out for letting things and people distract you from your business goals. Time out for excuses. Time to get out of your own way and get down to business. Time to stop sleeping on your God given gifts and talents. Time to finally realize the success you say you need, want and deserve, minus the migraine.

I invite you to learn the insights that have helped me quit my day job, spend more quality time with family, get out of debt, vacation when I want, be my own boss, do what I love and get paid very well to do it. What I share with you in the "Mind Your Business Lady" book has allowed me to grow my own profitable businesses as well as those of my Business Consulting Clients. It is filled with many of the goodies I share with my clients, in my courses and the amazing members of our Sistars Women's Empowerment Network. Which if you're not a part of our amazing network, visit us at **www.Sistars.org** to join us today Sis!

Let's not waste another moment, time to get to it. I pray you are blessed, empowered and successful in your business as you read through these pages. I thank all my readers, those who pre-ordered, who always support and believe in me and my dreams. YOU ROCK and I love you to life!

Women Entrepreneurs are killing it in the game right now! Why not you Sis? I don't care who doubted you, forgot about you, won't support you, what she said or he said. It's time to prove to yourself that you can do it, no matter who and no matter what.

It's time to Mind Your Business Lady!

CHAPTER 1

THE STRUGGLE IS REAL

Well hello readers and welcome to all of you wonderful purpose driven Women Entrepreneurs. Whether you are currently in business for yourself or aspiring to start, I am super excited to guide you on your journey through the **"Mind Your Business Lady"** Textbook, Workbook and/or Online Course. Let me be one of the first to say Congratulations to you on choosing to be your own boss and level up in your business. I am honored to be your Consultant, Instructor, Sister, Friend and Mentor along this awesome journey of Entrepreneurship so many of us have chosen. So without further ado let me introduce myself and tell you just a bit about my journey on the road to success.

My name is Cheryle Woods, born and raised in the Bay Area. East Oakland, California to be exact. I am an Author, Business Consultant and CEO of Sistars Women's Empowerment Network a.k.a. Sisters Inspiring Sisters To Achieve Real Success. Visit us at **www.Sistars.org** if you want to learn more about the organization. On the flip side, to my family and close friends I am a Wife, Mother, Stay At Home Grandmother, Eldest Daughter, Sister, Niece, Cousin, Friend that can be counted on and called on for almost anything my dear family needs. I love to do what makes my heart happy and my passion and purpose is simply using what God put in me to help others. And in between helping others I love to read, write, fish, skate, play and create music, perform spoken word, host my own radio shows, sing karaoke and travel with my family.

So as you can see I wear and juggle many hats. Trying to run a business, care for a family and still make time for yourself is not the easiest thing for anyone. Hence the title of this chapter, ladies the struggle is real! And best believe there are many a day when I would rather be simply doing nothing, reading a good book, spending a day on the water fishing, skating at the marina or just chilled out watching a good movie. Can anyone relate?

But let's keep it real, duty calls right. These bills are not going to pay themselves and after 20+years slaving away in Corporate America, there is no better feeling than working for myself, having the freedom to do what I love and as a bonus, getting paid to do it. I thank God every day for the blessing of being able to not just help so many others reach their business goals but to be living the life I have always dreamed about. I remember the days sitting in an office, sitting in cubicles, fighting through rush hour traffic in the S.F. Bay Area, stressed out of my mind, living paycheck to paycheck. I was living a real life nightmare that I just couldn't for the life of me seem to wake up from.

My God, I get sad just thinking about it. Here I was making millions for my bosses and they could care less about me, my wellbeing, my family or my bills. It was all about the bottom line for them. I was replaceable in their eyes and it was the worst day and the best day of my life when I finally quit for good! I have a strong faith in God and in my skills as an award winning leader for some of the top Fortune 500 corporations. As bad as it looked, I knew that I would be okay eventually.

Honestly, at the time I was scared out of my mind. I had no idea what my future held. I did know that if I could make all that money for them, spend all day working for and building someone else's business, then I could for sure do the same for my own.

"Yes the struggle is real, but it does not have to be permanent!"

In the process of finding my own way, God led me to help so many other women struggling in the same area of starting and/or growing their businesses. We were all in the process of learning that yes the struggle is real, but it does not have to be permanent. And just like that, Sistars Women's Empowerment Network was born and now the Mind Your Business Lady textbook, online course and workbook that will help you fire your boss if you're wanting out of your 9-5, turn your passion into profits and finally learn to use those God given gifts and talents to create wealth while serving others.

It took me over 20 years of selling my God given gifts for way less than I was worth before I finally got to a point where enough was enough and anymore would be too much. I was fed up! After a grueling year, struggling to survive in a toxic work environment, it seemed as I had no choice but to walk away from a career, from which I thought I would retire. I had been working in Corporate America since I was 14 years old. Years of working my way up the corporate ladder and honing my skills in the Technical and Sales Divisions of my Company would all come to an abrupt end.

I remember it like it was yesterday, even though I have been in business for myself for over 10 years now. There was a political push to write up our entire department for attendance issues, even though we were the only department who did not have a formal attendance policy. It was common practice to come in within 10 minutes of your start time and complete your shift within 10 minutes of your end time, whether it was 10 minutes early or 10 minutes late.

Our department, which provided technical assistance to our onsite technicians, was smack dab in the middle of a call center that was held to strict phone login schedules. So you can guess that our laid back tech work environment was hated on frequently. There came a time when the complaints reached upper management who wanted to retro-actively write up our entire department and HR got involved. This all came to a head on a Friday.

Now right is right and wrong is wrong, I have never been the one to keep quiet and not stand up for myself and those I care about. So after me going to bat for my department with upper management and HR, HR decided no one would be written up at all. However, a formal attendance policy would soon be written and put in place. After so many meetings it seemed as if we had been heard and finally recused of any wrongdoing. That is until I came into work on the next day which was a Saturday.

I was called into a meeting with a newly promoted supervisor and manager who had not worked Friday and had no clue which way was up. Can you believe these people tried to give me and others on my team a write up to sign for attendance, which of course I refused? Even after advising they speak with HR on Monday, here I sat in a conference room made for 2 people squeezed between 3 male managers who tried to force me to sign my life away.

Not only did I not sign it, but I left that job and office for good that day. First going out on stress leave for months, per my doctor's recommendation of course and then finally quitting for good.

"I was so uncomfortable in what used to be a comfortable situation"

Like I said before it was the worst and best day of my life. I just didn't know it then. If it had not been for God putting a fire under my butt where I was so uncomfortable in what used to be a comfortable situation, I would never have started my own business at all. Thank you God!

So what is *your story*? Don't be afraid to share it! It will help you, your business and those you are called to serve. Have you allowed yourself to stay too long in a "comfortable" situation? Are you allowing fear of the unknown to hold you stuck and stagnant, afraid to move on into your destiny? Are you so used to struggling that you can't see a way out and have put all your dreams and visions for being your own boss aside? Do you have a strong desire to start or grow your business but just simply do not know how? I am here to tell you, you are not alone. And you are in the right place to get the help you want and need. The right place to be able to do what you love, love what you do and get paid to do it.

As an Author, Business Consultant and CEO of Sistars Women's Empowerment Network and Mind Your Business Lady LLC, I teach purpose driven Women Entrepreneurs exactly how to use their God given gifts and talents to create wealth while serving others. It is my firm belief that every single one of us has God given gifts and talents that we are to use not just for our own benefits but to help others. I also know for a fact that God wants you to prosper, yes you! He says it plain and simple in my favorite bible verse, **Jeremiah 29:11, "For I know the plans I have for you," declares the Lord, "plans to prosper you and not to harm you, to give you a hope and a future."** So good news! If God himself wants you to prosper and to give you a hope and a future, then who are we to argue with God?

Now before we get into the meat and potatoes of the **"Mind Your Business Lady"** book, let's get clear on who this book/online course/workbook is intended to help.

"Mind Your Business Lady" is for the aspiring or current Woman Entrepreneur who:

- May be stuck in a dead end job or toxic work environment and wants to go into business for yourself

- Is tired of running in circles when it comes to starting or growing your business and needs a clear plan of action

- Has tried the freebies, webinars or even paid for the help but has gotten little to no results

- Knows she has a purpose and is ready to use her God given gifts and talents to create wealth

- Is struggling to get your idea or business off the ground, has shed enough blood, sweat and tears and is ready for a change

"Mind Your Business Lady" is <u>NOT</u> for the Woman Entrepreneur who:

- Is not serious about creating a successful business

- Is satisfied with not living out God's purpose for your life

- o Is not willing to put forth your best effort to work through the excuses, distractions and anything else holding you back

- o Wants a get rich quick scheme or an easy done for you solution

- o Is not willing to invest your time, energy and resources into building the business of your dreams

Now that you know for sure that the "**Mind Your Business Lady**" is for you, let's go over the layout and how you can get the most out of our time together.

1. Each Chapter of this MYBL Textbook has a corresponding Chapter in the Online Workbook for those enrolled in the Mind Your Business Lady Course. To get the most impact and to imbed what you have read in this Textbook, it is recommended that after reading each Textbook Chapter, you head on over to the Online Workbook and complete the work outlined there. If you have the book as a standalone, make sure you complete the Chapter Take-Aways and take note of what you will implement in your business.

2. For those of you who are also taking the "Mind Your Business Lady" Online Course, there are portions of this book that may be skipped over due to time constraints. It is highly recommended that you read this book in its entirety to best benefit your business growth. If you have yet to register for the Online Course you can do so by visiting **www.MindYourBusinessLady.com/Course**

3. Chapter 9 and Bonus Sections have resources and tools that I and my clients use to help grow our businesses. As of the date of this publication all resources, tools and apps are current and up to date. However, as things change we will update any changes in the MYBL Online Course Workbook and email links with updates. So make sure to stay connected.

Great! Again I am super happy and excited that you decided to join our Mind Your Business Lady family. As we endeavor on our individual journeys to success, it is no accident that you are reading this book and surely no accident that our paths have crossed. It is my life purpose to help others, to pour out what has been poured into me via years of education, experience and in working with some of the most amazing Powerhouse Women Entrepreneurs that are absolutely killing it in their respective industries. It does not matter how much you know or don't know, how much money you have or don't have, what skills you don't have or need to work on, **YOU DESERVE TO BE SUCCESSFUL!**

Let's be clear. No amount of luck can catapult you into an instant, successful and lucrative business. It is going to take some hard work, consistency, discipline and dedication. It is going to take you giving up some things and maybe even some people that are standing in your way of realizing the business of your dreams.

It is going to take some late nights and early mornings. It is going to mean saying no when you used to say yes and saying yes when you want to say no. It is going to mean giving yourself permission to take the time and energy out for yourself, to work on you and your business. It is going to take stepping out of your comfort zone, no matter how uncomfortable you may get.

It is going to take learning some new habits and letting go of some old ones. It is going to take you adopting an attitude and mindset that you will succeed no matter what it takes. That means staying true to what you say you want and following it up with focused action, no matter what it takes! Are you in?

Look at it this way. You have those looking for a get rich quick scheme that end up making zero and possibly getting scammed in the process. You have lottery winners, in fact statistics say more than 70%, who go broke only a few years after receiving their winnings. Then you have those who no matter their circumstances, no matter their age, no matter their perceived or actual disabilities, who worked hard at their goals and dreams and achieved massive success. Like Tyler Perry and Tiffany Haddish who both once were homeless living out of their cars and are now at the top of their fields in their respective careers. Or J.K. Rowling of the Harry Potter franchise, who secured her success while jobless, suffering from a failed marriage, a single mother on welfare. And of course we can't forget Oprah, media mogul, woman entrepreneur extraordinaire, who at a young age experienced abuse and poverty only to work hard and climb her way up to become the household name she is today.

I hear you though, don't think I don't. You are saying, "Now Cheryle I'm not nobody's Oprah" or "I don't have Tiffany's, Tyler's or J.K's skills or talents." WELL, GUESS WHAT, you don't have to! I am here to help you identify, extract and best utilize YOUR OWN God given gifts and talents.

I said it before and I will say it again, every single one of us has unique, God given gifts and talents that we are to use to create wealth while also serving others. No if's, and's, or but's about it. Not only do you deserve to be successful just as well as any of those famous people I mentioned above, but you have everything you need inside of you right now to make it happen. **YES YOU!!!**

So let's get started, your success cannot wait any longer. In order to succeed in business there are some basic things we need to identify about ourselves as women and as entrepreneurs first. Although the struggle is real, when we learn to keep it real with ourselves and evaluate our thoughts, gifts, talents and resources, we are destined for success!

CHAPTER 1 TAKE-AWAYS

- ➢ Don't be afraid to tell your story. Your struggle will help someone else get through theirs.
- ➢ What is your struggle in your business?
- ➢ Who is counting on you to succeed?
- ➢ WHY is it time for you to Mind Your Business Lady?

- ❖ Take a moment and write/type your story. What happened in your life that led you to starting your business? What obstacles have you overcame? How does your story relate to what your target audience is experiencing or struggling with right now? Tell your story!

CHAPTER 2

GOD'S GIFTS AND TALENTS

One of my greatest pleasures working with my clients is seeing them discover and blossom into their own unique God given gifts and talents. Too many times we as women, we as entrepreneurs, allow fear and doubt to overshadow the gifts that God has so lovingly given to each and every one of us. Or we allow our vision to get clouded or misdirected by looking at and focusing on the wrong things. Which is why it is a must that you learn to **Mind Your Business Lady**!

Here are just a few ways our vision can become clouded or misdirected:

1. **Focusing on the gifts, talents or blessings of others**

2. **Being too critical of ourselves, expecting perfection**

3. **Too much social media, reality tv, even the evening news**

Truly I could go on and on but I will stop at those 3 points. Our job is to recognize those things that may be clouding our vision for the amazing lives God wants for us. We must eliminate any and everything that is not in alignment with all the **good things:**

- ✓ Running that successful business
- ✓ Serving others
- ✓ 6-7 figures in your bank account
- ✓ Quitting your 9-5
- ✓ Paying off your debt
- ✓ Sending your kids to college not worrying about the cost
- ✓ Taking care of your parents and family
- ✓ Funding that organization/cause
- ✓ Taking those dream vacations
- ✓ Crossing those items off your bucket list
- ✓ And whatever else God has placed on your heart when you envision that successful, amazing, Woman Entrepreneur you are aiming to be.

In this chapter, you will learn how to identify and develop your own God given gifts and talents, as well as how those gifts and talents align with your purpose in life. And don't worry if you have little to no clue what your gifts and talents are or if you are struggling to find your purpose as it relates to your business. Along with the exercises in the "Mind Your Business Lady" Workbook, we will journey into the discovery or re-discovery of both.

So what is purpose anyway?

Is it something we are innately born with or something that we somehow stumble upon along life's journey as we grow and experience new things, people and situations? The answer: it is both. Some of us come out of the womb knowing without a doubt what we are great at and what we were born to do. You have child prodigies who are graduating college before they hit their teen years, singers like the late great Michael Jackson who probably sang his first words and moonwalked his first steps, and other brilliant, gifted and talented children that may even be in your own family, that you were blessed to birth or even you. Those born with significant gifts and talents are no different from those who learn or discover theirs later on in life. The only difference between the two is timing. And one is no better than the other. For some of us it is our very struggles, situations and experiences that are necessary for our purpose to become clear and who better to help someone else through something than the one who has already been through it.

> *"Fact: We were all created for a purpose and we all have God given gifts and talents to help us fulfill our purpose in life while also serving others."*

We all have God given gifts and talents to help us fulfill our purpose in life while also serving others. Take a moment to think about some of the things you have needed help with or struggled with in life. Who was able to help you through, who did you turn to for help, guidance or advice? Was it someone who had no clue of your pain, problem or issue or was it someone that you felt for whatever reason could relate to what you were experiencing? Maybe it was a professional who had knowledge on how to help you through education or a layman who could help you because they had experienced the same or similar. The fact is, either through what we learn or experience, our purpose becomes clearer. Then we are better equipped to help and serve others.

Pay attention to the patterns in your life and know that everything happens for a reason. Good or bad, things happen to grow us or show us. Situations that are painful or uncomfortable are meant to grow us in an area we may need clarity, healing or understanding.

While situations we struggle through are there to show us what we are really made of after all. It shows us that we are stronger, more knowledgeable and resourceful than we give ourselves credit for or think. I call it our "pat yourself on the back moments." When you can't help but smile after it's all said and done. When you're in awe of God's grace and mercy, and proud of yourself for overcoming that challenge or perhaps helping someone else do the same.

Your purpose may be humanitarian in nature, helping those less fortunate. Like feeding/clothing the homeless. Or providing resources for single parents. Maybe it is guiding and empowering the youth. Or fostering children, being an advocate for those dealing with some real tough issues. You find yourself constantly concerned with or seeking to promote human welfare.

Your purpose in life may revolve around nature and caring for the planet.

Your purpose may be visionary, creating new ideas, dynamic thoughts and technologies.

Your purpose may be creative, using your talents and skills to create works of art, cook amazing meals, make new products, inventions, crafts and designs.

Your purpose may be spiritual, ministering, prophesying, and sharing the word and love of God with others.

Your purpose may revolve around love, inspiration, devotion, providing for others, connecting with others, leading, teaching, writing, singing, dancing, acting, speaking, motivating, encouraging, listening to and praying for others.

Your purpose is anything that makes you happy to do it. It is a gift that you can share to help others in some magical way.

So how do we find our purpose and how do we identify our own unique God given gifts and talents? Start by asking yourself these three questions:

1. What is it I love to do even if I'm not getting paid to do it?

2. What is it that others are always asking my help with?

3. What is it that others are always complimenting me on?

For me I absolutely love to write and teach others how to do something they may be struggling with in life and business. My friends, family, colleagues and clients are always asking for my help in writing their books and running their businesses.

I am always complimented on my gift of encouraging, inspiring and empowering others through motivational speaking, my books and poems, spoken word and just in everyday interactions with everyone I meet. In a nutshell I know my purpose is to inspire and encourage others to succeed in life through my gifts and talents of writing, speaking and teaching.

There are so many differing gifts and talents that we all possess. Yes even you. Especially you! As a matter of fact I will go so far to say that you have multiple God given gifts and talents that you can and should be using to create wealth while serving others.

Let's take a moment and look at just a few Bible verses that speak on our God given gifts and talents. I am definitely a believer in His Word. And if you are experiencing any doubt or fear when it comes to identifying and embracing your own gifts and talents, simply take some time out during your day, to repeat these out loud until it gets in your spirit. What we speak has no choice but to manifest in your life. And Honey, I know from experience that God's Word is powerful and does not come back void. So speak it, believe it and receive it, amen!

- "We have different gifts, according to the grace given to each of us. If your gift is prophesying, then prophesy in accordance with your faith; if it is serving, then serve; if it is teaching, then teach; if it is to encourage, then give encouragement; if it is giving, then give generously; if it is to lead, do it diligently; if it is to show mercy, do it cheerfully." – Romans 12: 6-8

- "Do you see someone skilled in their work? They will serve before kings; they will not serve before officials of low rank." – Proverbs 22:29

- "For we are God's handiwork, created in Christ Jesus to do good works, which God prepared in advance for us to do." – Ephesians 2:10

- "All who are skilled among you are to come and make everything the Lord has commanded." – Exodus 35:10

- "Every good and perfect gift is from above, coming down from the Father of the heavenly lights, who does not change like shifting shadows." – James 1:17

> "Each of you should use whatever gift you have received to serve others, as faithful stewards of God's grace in its various forms. If anyone speaks, they should do so as one who speaks the very words of God. If anyone serves, they should do so with the strength God provides, so that in all things God may be praised through Jesus Christ. To him be the glory and the power for ever and ever. Amen." – 1 Peter 4:10-11

And last but definitely not least is the Bible verse that reminds us all that we should never hide our gifts and talents. It is one of my favorites, "The Parable of the Talents."

Back in biblical times a talent referred to a single weight worth a large sum of money (it is said one talent would be equal to approximately 1 million dollars today). When we read the parable we must not always think literally, but read with our hearts, not simply our minds. This verse is definitely speaking to our own God given gifts and talents and how we choose to use them. Those who have ears, let them hear.

"The Parable of the Talents – Matthew 25:14-30"

> *For it will be like a man going on a journey, who called his servants and entrusted them to his property. To one he gave five talents, to another two, to another one, to each according to his ability. Then he went away. He who had received the five talents went at once and traded with them, and he made five talents more. So*

also he who had the two talents made two talents more. But he who had received the one talent went and dug in the ground and hid his master's money.

- *Now after a long time the master of those servants came and settled accounts with them. And he who had received the five talents came forward, bringing five talents more, saying, 'Master, you delivered to me five talents; here, I have made 5 talents more.' His master said to him, 'Well done, good and faithful servant. You have been faithful over a little; I will set you over much. Enter into the joy of your master.' And he also who had the two talents came forward, saying, 'Master, you delivered to me two talents; here, I have made two talents more.' His master said to him, 'Well done, good and faithful servant. You have been faithful over a little; I will set you over much. Enter into the joy of your master.'*

- *He also who had received the one talent came forward saying, 'Master, I knew you to be a hard man, reaping where you did not sow, and gathering where you scattered no seed, so I was afraid, and I went and hid your talent in the ground. Here, you have what is yours.' But his master answered him, 'You wicked and slothful servant! You knew that I reap where I have not sown and gather where I scattered no seed? Then you ought to have invested my money with the bankers, and at my coming I should have received what was my own with interest. So take the talent from him and give it to the one who has the ten talents. For to everyone who has will more be given, and he who has not, even what he has will be taken away. And cast the worthless servant into the outer darkness. In that place there will be weeping and gnashing of teeth.'*

My God! I get chills whenever I read that parable. It is my sincere prayer that we do not allow fear to cause us to hide our God given gifts and talents. That by God's strength and grace we continue to use them to serve others. That we, when we finally face our heavenly Father, are able to hear those beautiful words, "Well done, my good and faithful servant. Enter into the joy of your master."

"Why is it so important for you to have a successful business?"

This is a question I so often ask my clients who are having trouble figuring out *how* they can use their God given gifts and talents to create wealth while serving others. **"Why is it so important for you to have a successful business?"** This answers the big question of *"What is your 'WHY'?"* Why must you succeed? Why did you choose to go into business for yourself? Why did you choose this particular business? Why is it that you absolutely cannot fail?

And to take it a step further, I say let's answer all 5 W's.

Who, What, When, Where and Why.

- ***Who*** is counting on you to succeed and who will suffer if you don't?
- ***What*** does success look like to you, what will it help you accomplish?
- ***When*** will you start working on your success? Now, tomorrow, next year?
- ***Where*** will success take you? Where will you work, where will you live, vacation?
- ***Why*** is it so important for you to have a successful business? Why is it so necessary that you keep going, keep growing and cannot give up?

These questions are also repeated in the Chapter Take-Away at the end of this chapter. It is just that important that you dig deep and get the answers to these questions at the forefront of your mind. Commit these answers to memory. Write them down where you can see and read them every day. If you are still transitioning from your 9-5 place them on your desk or workspace. If you drive to work place them on your dashboard. Put them on your mirror in the bathroom, by your bed or in your kitchen on the refrigerator.

There is no excuse to not knowing the answers to these questions as it will make or break the success of your business. It's like digging a hole but not knowing why you are digging it. How energetic, how dedicated, how much oomph are you going to put into digging a hole if someone just passes you a shovel and says "dig" but doesn't give you a reason why? You will get tired, frustrated and sooner or later you will quit. But what if someone says I am going to pay you $10,000 to dig this hole, or you will strike oil if you dig this hole, or water to supply your entire village, or precious metals like gold, diamonds or silver? Will your motivation to get it done change?

Guess what? I bet not only will you keep digging, you may even enlist others to help and develop tools and techniques to make the digging easier and more productive. And when you do get tired, when the digging gets rough, when there seems to be no water, or oil, or gold or the $10,000 starts to seem like chump change compared to all your effort and you simply want to quit, you won't. You will shovel one more time, you will take a break and try again and again because you know WHY you are digging and you know the reward will be worth it. So it is the same in your business, your hard work will pay off. So keep digging sister, keep digging.

MONEY VS PASSION…..THE VALUE IN SERVING

Learning how to do what you love and love what you do, while getting paid to do it is what I teach my Business Consulting Clients. But to keep it real, money cannot and should not be your driving force. There is immense value in serving those who you are called to help. Whether your business is product based or service based, the solutions that you are providing to your clients are priceless.

Yes we place a price tag on our products and services but in no way should money be your motivating factor for doing what you do. In fact I have turned down clients and investors whose sole reason for wanting to get into business or invest in my own was to strictly get rich. My clients are all purpose driven Women Entrepreneurs who have a non-monetary, heart felt reason for doing what they do and I love it.

Money is a tool that we are to use, not our main goal to attain as so many think. I didn't start my consulting business or writing books because I wanted to make a million dollars. No on the contrary it was my love for helping others and my love for getting my thoughts and ideas on paper in a way that could encourage others. In fact, when I started out so many years ago I would do it for free. When you are doing what you love, you would do it even if you were not getting paid to do it.

Now I'm not saying go around offering all your gifts and talents for free, no. What I am saying is that you should be running your business because you are passionate about it, passionate about your craft, your skills and mostly passionate about those you serve.

Trust and believe! When you are using your God given gifts and talents to serve others, the money will come. God wants you to prosper, He is not a God of lack and He will always provide what we need. You are a child of the King and never ever have I seen the righteous forsaken nor his seed begging for bread. Trust and believe that God gave you those gifts for a reason and your gift will make room for you.

So continue to hone in on your God given gifts and talents. Study, practice, volunteer. Find different ways to express them through service of others and then find ways to monetize that service. You are the solution to someone's problem, what you have inside of you right now is the very answer to someone's prayers. And remember practice makes perfect.

Don't forget the "Parable of the Talents", your gifts and talents are never to be hidden. We all know the saying, 'If you don't use it you will lose it".

CHAPTER 2 TAKE-AWAYS

- **Every single one of us has a God given gift or talent. Many of you have multiple gifts and talents.**
- **It is okay to use those gifts and talents to create wealth for yourself and your family while you serve others.**
- **You are created for a purpose. Stop hiding and being afraid to share your gifts!**

DO THIS NOW!

Answer the 5 W's - Who, What, When, Where and Why.

- ❖ **Who** is counting on you to succeed and who will suffer if you don't?
- ❖ **What** does success look like to you, what will it help you accomplish?
- ❖ **When** will you start working on your success? Now, tomorrow, next year?

❖ ***Where*** will success take you? Where will you work, where will you live, vacation?
❖ ***Why*** is it so important for you to have a successful business? Why is it so necessary that you keep going, keep growing and cannot give up?

Chapter 3

"MIND" YOUR BUSINESS LADY, IT PAYS

In this Chapter we are going to tackle one of the biggest things that has the power to make or break your business, which is MINDSET. What you think about your ability to succeed. How you think about money. What you are telling yourself internally about your own skills, gifts and talents. As well as any deep-rooted thought patterns that you may have learned in childhood and throughout the years. These all affect your mindset.

Mindset is powerful. It forms your thoughts, which forms your words, which forms your actions. It is the difference between being able to take the risks necessary to achieve success in your business versus playing it safe. The wrong mindset allows fear to paralyze you into staying "safe" and stagnant getting little to nothing done at all. It is the difference between having a successful, lucrative business versus a business that you treat like a hobby with sporadic sales and income. A positive mindset brings about prosperity in all you do, while a negative mindset only brings about lack; lack of motivation, lack of inspiration and lack of finances.

Let's talk about some of the bi-products of a negative mindset, which I call the **3 Big Dream Killers**. Dream killers are things we tell ourselves (or allow others to tell us) that we use as excuses as to why we cannot start, grow and ultimately succeed in our business.

Dream Killer #1 – No Time

Have you ever said to yourself, ***"I just don't have the time to start/grow my business?"*** Or to write that book, proposal, business plan or to plan that event or complete that project. While it is true that as Women Entrepreneurs we all have busy lives, it is also true that we make the time for the things we really want. The fact is saying or thinking that we have no time is just one of many excuses we use due to fear.

Yes, I will be the first to say that as a Woman Entrepreneur, we wear many hats. When I decided to start my own business, I was working full time, attending school, volunteering at church, while also trying to be the best wife and mother I could. Many of you are struggling to juggle even more than that. Ladies, I know the struggle is real and time is something that is a precious commodity. Yet we all have the same 24 hours in a day, right? It is what we choose to do with those 24 hours that sets apart those who will succeed and those who will succumb to **Dream Killer #1 – No Time**.

I invite you to seriously take account of all you do throughout your day. How and where are you spending your time? Are you making the most of your time, being practical about writing goals, sticking to a schedule and prioritizing your time? Or are you being wasteful with your time, spending hours surfing the internet or on social media? Are you focusing on busy work like checking unimportant emails? How much time do you spend watching reality TV or gossiping on the phone about people and things that aren't your business? Do you have a habit of oversleeping or daydreaming your life away? On what and where are you spending and/or wasting your time?

You may know exactly where your time is being wasted away. For others it may be necessary to take a day or two to actually log to the minute what you are doing and when. It is time to take back your time. Time to eliminate the things you know are wasting your precious time. It is time to become that awesome, Woman Entrepreneur who is on top of her game at all times. It is time to Mind Your Business Lady!

There are so many ways we can take back or even make time where we may have thought there was none. For those still working those 9-5's your breaks and lunchtimes are a gold mine. You may think "oh no I am just so tired after working that all I want to do is eat, rest or kick up my feet on my breaks." That is understandable, some work can be draining.

But what if instead of taking the full hour or both breaks eating and relaxing that you dedicated 30 minutes to starting or growing your business? Or even work on your business while you eat? That would add 2.5 - 5 hours during a 40 hour work week that you dedicate to your business. And while that does not sound like much I guarantee you that two and a half hours of focused action is much better than 0 hours of no action at all. So take charge of your time and make it count.

Maybe you are a mom, which I know from experience is a never ending job. For the younger kids, regularly scheduled nap times will be your best friend. Enlist the help of trusted family or friends to watch the kids for an hour or two. Get with other moms in your circle to set up rotating play dates, where one or two moms deal with the kids while the others work. And for the school aged kids, after school programs are great for their development and frees up time for you to work on your business. If you have older or adult children like I do, why not enlist their help with running or growing your business? You may be surprised at the skills they have that can help you in your business.

I tell you some of you are sitting on an untapped gold mine when it comes to the many skills, gifts and talents your children have. Creating your YouTube channel, taking photos/videos, navigating social media. This new generation is super tech savvy so take advantage of that while also building a bond with your children and teaching them your business as well.

When it comes to freeing up time to work on your business, there are so many creative ideas that you can find. It is not only doable, but absolutely necessary. What can you eliminate, whose help can you enlist, what tasks/chores can you delegate? How can you find ways to make time for your business?

Dream Killer #2 – No Money

"I just don't have the money" - Dreaded Dream Killer #2. This is one that I hear quite often when speaking with women struggling to start or grow their business. And one that I prove time and time again that 99% of the time just is not true. I have helped many of my Business Consulting clients overcome this dream killer and you can do the same.

There is an assumption that you need a huge amount of money to start your business or grow your business to the next level. Many think there is the need to apply for and receive huge loans or grants. This is far from the truth. And while yes it does take money to make money there are so many creative solutions to funding your dream, that we cannot allow Dream Killer #3 to even plant a seed and take root in our minds.

Usually those who are struggling with the "No Money" excuse are dealing with one or more financial hurdles. I use the word "excuse" because that is exactly what they are, excuses we use so we don't have to take accountability for our finances and/or lack thereof. These hurdles can be broken down into 3 categories; **poor money management, lack of resources and situational stagnation**. Let's discuss the definition of each and the creative solutions we can apply to resolve them.

Poor Money Management

Poor money management starts with poor habits and thoughts surrounding and money. Poor money management skills are something we learn early in life, as far back as our childhood. It may start with how we manage our allowances, our paychecks from our first summer jobs or even money we may have been given as gifts or earned from odd jobs, etc.

Some of us were taught the value of saving or adopted the saving bug from our parents and caregivers. Perhaps money was scarce which resulted in the habit of saving and cherishing the money we did come across. On the other hand, you may have learned habits of excess spending with little to no regard for budgeting. If money was never an issue growing up, came easy to you or you came from a well off family and you never had to worry about where your next dollar was coming from, this may affect your lack of saving or habits of frivolous spending.

More than likely we inherit our money habits from our parents or those who raised us. So if mom and dad were great savers then we develop the habit of saving. However if our parents were spendthrifts or constantly in debt, we may follow in those same footsteps. As we grow into adulthood and real life begins (the rent, mortgage, car notes, utility bills, credit cards, hospital bills, insurance, etc.) now those habits have a huge impact on our finances and money management skills.

As a young adult in my early 20's, I remember an incident partying with my cousins and one of my cousins said she had to go home early as she had bills to pay in the morning. All of us made fun of her, called her a party pooper and were sad that she was ending our fun night out early. A few years later that same cousin was buying her first home with her good credit while the rest of us were still paying rent and in debt. If only we had paid attention and realized the importance of paying bills on time, saving and the great money management skills my cousin possessed.

So what's the solution? How do you overcome your poor money management skills? The answer is replacing those poor money management skills with new habits that will work *for* you and not against you. Learn budgeting skills, saving, paying your bills on time, reviewing/repairing your credit, and the art of not overspending. Also finding ways to make your money work for you via smart investing, credit card rewards incentives, couponing and other measure that can bring in a great return to your pockets.

Taking full responsibility for learning to manage your money will eliminate the late fees, stress of debt, and high interest rates or even being turned down for loans and funding. Educating yourself on how to best manage the money you do have and getting expert help if needed is a must. Manage the money you have to free up the money you need to grow your business.

Lack of resources

Yet another hurdle that goes hand in hand with ***Dream Killer #2-*** "***No Money***" is lack of resources. You may simply be stretched to the max as many are today when it comes to finances. You may be working or in school or a single mom and the money or income you have is already stretched thin. You may not have enough after paying bills to save or invest. The good news is when you do take the steps in this "**Mind Your Business Lady**" guide to start or grow your business in the right way, your finances and resources will increase as a result. But what do you do in the meantime? How do you find the money to start or grow your business when you have little to no money left after paying bills and providing for your family?

The fact is you can't squeeze juice from a dry lemon. So if you find that you are living paycheck to paycheck, robbing Peter to pay Paul, drowning in debt payments and having more month at the end of your paycheck rather than more paycheck at the end of your month, then it is time to get creative. It is time to find creative ways to fund your dream, invest in your business and yourself. The ultimate goal is to increase your resources where you can obtain more money, more help and services you need to grow your business.

Problem: "I need money!" To make more money we need what I call *Creative Funding* sources. Creative Funding is simply obtaining money to start or grow your business using non-traditional income sources. There are a million ways we can make more money that we can use to start and grow our business today. A few of my favorite ways that have worked for me and my clients are:

- Flea market/Garage Sales/Online Sales of items you no longer use or need
- Focus Groups and Paid Studies
- Secret Shopping
- Recycling/Reselling items
- Weekend/Overnight Daycare
- Lyft/Uber/DoorDash

- Providing Services on Upwork and Fiverr
- Affiliate Marketing
- Middle Man Marketing: charge a finder's fee to connect a buyer with a seller
- Get paid to refer others through referral programs
- Use your God given skills to pay the bills
- *Check out Chapter 9 "Biz On A Budget" for more tips

Problem: "I need help!" To get more help, we simply ask those close to us and those who'd be willing to volunteer their time. Our spouse/partner, children, family and friends who support and believe in us and our dreams are an excellent resource to get help in our business. A closed mouth does not get fed and the Bible tells us "we have not because we ask not." You would be surprised the amount of people you already have around you who have the skills, desire and time to help you grow your business and will do so for free. Just because they love you and believe in your God given gifts and talents.

I am so grateful to my mother who is amazingly skilled at so many things and my sister who is an artist/animator/graphic designer and are always willing and able to help me out in my many business endeavors. And my husband, daughter and brother who play a huge part in my success as well. My entire family is very supportive whether it is through physical help, purchasing my books, sending me referrals, advice, prayer or simply sharing a post or two. Trust, it may be the people you least expect who will be willing to help you, just ask!

To get the services you need we either barter our own services with others who provide the services that we need or we utilize low cost services or even free services. Bartering is a great way to get the services or even products we need to start or grow our business. Perhaps you know a great copywriter or photographer or makeup artist and you are a great marketer. All you have to do is offer to exchange services with that person. You do something you're great at for them and in turn they do something they're great at for you. And please make sure you give them credit, thanks and appreciation for their awesome work by posting, sharing and referring their work with your network and ask they do the same for you. This way everyone wins!

Situational Stagnation

Situational Stagnation is any *real* circumstance that leaves you feeling stuck and is the <u>*actual cause*</u> of you falling under the category of **Dream Killer #2 – No Money**. It makes you believe there is no way out of your situation and that you will be stuck in it forever. Situational Stagnation causes you to experience an attitude of defeat as you may not see an immediate solution to get the money you need to fund your business.

Situational Stagnation is common in those who may be suffering from physical/mental disabilities or illness, experiencing homelessness, a minor or elderly with little income/resources, receiving government assistance, unemployed, a new mom or full-time caretaker for a loved one. It is any life situation that keeps you stagnant and not moving forward in your business.

The secret to overcoming Situational Stagnation is simply knowing and believing that things will get better and you can be successful in spite of your current situation even while you are living through it. In fact new ideas, businesses and solutions are often born as a result of you finding new ways to overcome it. For example, who better to start an organization or program to help the homeless than someone who has lived through it?

The key is to not lose hope and do what you can now with what you have now. If you are disabled, work within your limits, ask for donations to fund your dream and enlist the help of others to do what you cannot to grow your business.

If you are unemployed, this means you have all the time in the world to create your own job by doing side jobs and using your God given gifts and talents offering your services full time.

If you are on a fixed income, a new mom, or a caretaker who may spend most of your time caring for others, you can make money to fund your business by getting paid to do what you are already doing. Ask yourself, "What am I doing now that someone would pay me to do?" If you are cooking meals you can prepare an extra casserole or dish that can be heated in the oven to sell. If you are picking up kids from school you can offer to pick up or drop off others in your kids' school for a fee. If you are shopping there are apps that will pay you to shop for others. If you are great at couponing you can stock up on items and resell them online for a profit, or even charge others to teach them to coupon.

The point is that no matter the reason for **Dream Killer #2 – No Money**, you can find creative ways to fund your business. All hope is not lost. You can get to the point where you no longer have to worry about where or how you will find the money you need to invest in your business. Start where you are with what you have and invest at the level that you are at.

*Perhaps you only have $25 to invest this week, invest it wisely in something that will make you more money. $25 invested in ingredients to make 10 cakes that you sell for $10 each will make you $100 or a $75 profit. Now instead of $25 you have $100 to reinvest in your business. This same rule can be applied no matter your gift or talent. Ask yourself what product or service can I sell/provide right now that will bring in cash to fund my dream. The possibilities are truly endless.

*This is only an example and not intended to guarantee any specific results. Research the prices, time and actual investments for your specific gift and/or talent.

Dream Killer #3 – Lack Of Skills/Perfect Patty Syndrome

Now on to the last and most dreaded **Dream Killer #3 – Lack of skills and on the flip side the need to be perfect**. This Dream Killer is a double edged sword. No matter what side you may fall on it will hurt you and your business. On one side you have those who feel like they are not good enough that they lack the skills, talent or gifts that someone would pay them for at all. The other side is the exact opposite, those Perfect Patties who just have to have everything exactly right before they make a move forward in starting/growing their business.

Both sides are driven by fear of what other people will think, yet the results are the same. No one will *buy* their products and services simply because no one ever gets to *see* their services or products. These thoughts or similar invade their minds:

"I'm just not good enough."

"She is so talented I could never do that."

"My ideas will never work."

"Nobody will pay me for this."

"I have to get this perfectly right."

"I can't share this offer until xyz."

"I just need one more product and then I will post the offer link."

"Maybe if I add this or change that one last time it will be ready."

Have you told yourself any of the statements above or something similar? Has any of these thoughts stopped you from moving forward in your business? How many times have you doubted that your gifts and talents were good enough, that you were good enough? How long have you allowed the fear of what other people think or will say or will do or won't do to stop you? How long has it been that you've allowed your dreams and ideas to be killed before you even gave them a chance?

Dream Killer #3 is overcome by mastering the thoughts and beliefs in your head. Overcoming it takes a major mind shift and commitment to **"Do it anyway!"**

Even if you are scared, do it anyway!

Even if you feel you aren't good enough, do it anyway!

Even if you think your work could be better, do it anyway!

Even if you feel there is a better product or service out there, do it anyway!

Keep your dreams alive by just taking one step, then another, and another. And guess what pretty soon you will be running your business like the Boss Lady you have always been but just didn't realize. The only way any of these **3 Dream Killers – "No Time, No Money and Lack of Skills/Perfect Patty Syndrome"** can kill your dreams is if you lay down and let them. It's time to get up and get to it and Mind Your Business Lady….it pays!

DISTRACTIONS, NAYSAYERS, DOUBTERS AND NON-SUPPORTERS

I can't end this chapter without touching on a topic that often affects so many Women Entrepreneurs in my network and in general. And that is the distractions, naysayers, doubters and non-supporters. If you have not encountered either of these then you must be living on a deserted island or are the real life Superwoman in the flesh.

Distractions come in so many forms and are just the ways, people and things the devil uses to attempt to take our focus off of God's plans for our lives and businesses.

Naysayers and doubters are those who tell you what you can't do and why you can't do it. Often it is because deep down they don't think they can do it either and refuse to even think you can be the exception.

Non-supporters are usually family and friends who you love and want more than anything for them to root for you but for whatever reason they don't. Please don't take this personal, you never know what others are dealing with in their lives that may be the reason they can't or won't support you.

All of the above can derail your focus and undermine your success if you give them any attention at all. The GOOD NEWS is what others think or don't think about you is really none of your business. And when I teach and preach "**Mind Your Business Lady"** this is one of the things I'm talking about...which is remaining laser focused on your own dreams and goals no matter who and no matter what!

The key to *defeating distractions* is recognizing them for exactly what they are. Anything that takes your focus away from what you know you should be doing to start or grow your business is a distraction. We must be very careful with distractions as sometimes they can be a lot of fun and feel good in the moment. Perhaps you are working on a deadline and you get a call from your friends to meet them at the bar for drinks. Or maybe you are posting an update on your Facebook page but end up scrolling your timeline and watching funny videos for the next hour.

Distractions come in many forms as you can see. So recognize them for what they are and learn to just say no and nip it in the bud. You have to be disciplined and know that all your hard work will pay off and then you can reward yourself with free time after. You have to learn to put business before pleasure if you are seriously ready to Mind Your Business Lady.

Naysayers and doubters can be disguised as loved ones, co-workers, bosses, even spouses/partners. They don't hate you, they just don't believe in your vision because they can't see your vision. These are the people you have to be firm and direct with. Tell them, "Thank you for your opinion, but no thank you. I got this!" Then proceed to focus on your goals and succeed anyway. Remember it's not important what he say, she say, they say. What did God say? Well, He says, "I can do all things through Christ who strengthens me." Philippians 4:13 and who can argue with God?

Like the naysayers and doubters, *non-supporters* can also come in the forms of family, friends and loved ones. In fact they usually are. Non-supporters are the ones who don't share your posts, don't buy your products or services and don't attend your events. The non-supporters in your life don't support for many different reasons but I will focus on the only one that matters. They don't support you because they are not your dream client or ideal customer.

Yes there may be a few haters scattered here and there because they are just not happy for your success but I refuse to allow you to focus on them. What other people think or say about you is not your business. So in the spirit of the "Mind Your Business Lady" book and series we will only do just that, mind our business. Any energy you even think about wasting on addressing any of the distractions, naysayers, doubters and non-supporters, I want you to refocus that energy back on your business.

It's time to get excited about your dreams and using your God given gifts and talents to create wealth while serving others. You should be feeling like a kid in a candy store when you think about your business and the success that lies ahead. You should have a list of business goals that are S.M.A.R.T. Goals. Specific, Measurable, Attainable, Realistic and Time Bound. Write them down, tweak them if necessary, memorize them, and make them into a song if you need to. And when you accomplish one of your business goals or hit a milestone (no matter how big or small) always reward yourself. Take a break, get a massage, go for a movie or dinner, whatever way you want to tell yourself, "Great job!" Without breaking the bank of course.

One last thing before we wrap up chapter 3. When it comes to mindset, to staying focused, to being able to consistently, **"Mind Your Business Lady"**, there are **"5 Daily Practices"** I recommend you do on the daily. It will help your business and help you achieve the ultimate success you need, want and deserve. Doing these things daily will allow you to eliminate the dream killers in your life.

1. **Prayer** – Take time out every day and every night to talk to God about your business, your goals, your fears, your dreams, and your struggles. Ask Him to lead you in the way that seems right and pleasing to Him. And don't forget to give Him thanks for all He has already done, is doing and has yet to do in your life, in the lives of your loved ones and of course in your business.
2. **Daily Affirmations** – These are crucial to your ultimate success as well as mastering your mindset. Positive affirmations that you read/speak aloud daily have the power to shape your world. By His words God created all that we see now in the physical. Try it, I promise it works.
3. **Journaling** – Keeping a journal of your thoughts, the high and low points of your day, your conversations with God are a way to download all that may be on your mind at

the end of the day. It also is a great way to capture those brilliant ideas and dreams. You should do this daily and keep it where you can get to it easily (I keep mine on the nightstand by my bed as I often awake in the middle of the night with inspired ideas). And make sure to go back and read what you wrote, you will see that issues were resolved, prayers answered and ideas/thoughts are now your reality.

4. **Biz Support System** – I can't stress enough how important it is to have a support system of those who believe in you and your vision for your business. It's great to have friends. But when those friends are also business owners who not only understand your struggles and thought processes but can also lend valuable advice, everything looks so much brighter. You realize you are not alone, you gain insight into best practices for your business and you gain lifelong relationships and mentors who truly want to help and see you succeed. No crabs in the bucket syndrome.*

5. **Networking** - Meeting up with like-minded individuals both online and offline is a bonus that is just so fun and worthwhile. You never know who you are going to meet that will potentially become a client, partner, referral source, friend or all of the above. Get out there and speak to people at networking events, in your community, and even online.

*If you have yet to find your own Biz Support System, I invite you to join the Sistarhood at www.Sistars.org

Sisters Inspiring Sisters To Achieve Real Success a.k.a. Sistars Women's Empowerment Network is all about providing Women Entrepreneurs like you with the Network, Platform and Training to grow your business. We are a community of supportive, successful women in business who are a blessing to so many and each other.

I cannot say this enough, *"**Mind Your Business Lady**"*...it pays. In this chapter we have covered the basics of Mindset which is such an important part of growing a successful business. We covered the 3 Dream killers and how to overcome them. We dove into the many distractions trying to take away our focus from working on our business. And we listed 5 Daily Practices that you should be doing to stay on top of your game as amazing, empowered and successful Women Entrepreneurs. Now the most important part, is putting all these things into action!

CHAPTER 3 TAKE-AWAYS

- **Beware of the Big 3 Dream Killers, they only have the power you give them.**
- **Eliminate the distractions that are stealing your time.**
- **Ignore the haters, doubters, non-supporters and naysayers and Mind Your Business Lady!**

 **DO THIS NOW!**

- Make a list of the "5 Daily Practices" you will put in place. What will you pray? What are your affirmations? What time of day/evening will you journal? Who is in your Biz Support System? When/where will you network?

****Chapter 4 Disclaimer****

Before we dive into Chapter 4, "Legally Speaking, Dot Your i's & Cross Your t's" we must emphasize that in no way does the information contained serve as a substitute for legal counsel and doing your own due diligence.

The information contained in Chapter 4 serves merely as a guide to lead you in the direction of making the best, informed decisions about your business. Just as each of us as Women Entrepreneurs are different so are the needs of each individual business.

Please take the time to consult with a licensed and certified professional before making any final decisions about how to best structure and legally protect your particular business and assets.

Chapter 4

LEGALLY SPEAKING, DOT YOUR i'S & CROSS YOUR t'S

Before we go any further we must make sure we are on the right track to achieve the ultimate success that we all need, want and deserve in our business. And in order to do that we must go back to the basics. There are certain steps that as business owners, as Women Entrepreneurs we must all take to ensure the legality, protection and ultimate direction of our business. This is where we separate those who just have a hobby from those who are running successful, lucrative businesses. In this chapter, **"Dotting Your i's & Crossing Your t's"**, we will discuss the importance of making your business legal and help you to set it up with the proper licenses, certifications and registrations.

The Business Plan

One thing I ask all of my clients is, "Do you have a business plan?" The most common answer I receive from both new and seasoned entrepreneurs is a flat out, "No." They have no business plan and most, like me when I first started out didn't think it was absolutely necessary. If you're like most of my clients, you are thinking you just don't need it, which is far from the truth.

A **business plan** is a document that outlines the current and future objectives of your business. So why do you need a business plan? You may just be starting out and are eager to get started getting your product or service out to the public and making those sales, so you put it on the backburner. Or you may have been in business for quite some time and haven't felt the need for it all this time, so why now? If you don't already have one, then it is in the best interest of you and your business to take the time to get it done ASAP. There are many reasons creating a business plan is necessary and even beneficial for your business. Here are just a few:

- Funding - to obtain new loans, investors, grants, etc.
- A business plan is your roadmap to grow your business
- It contains your budget and operating procedures to keep you on track
- It is a clear layout of your vision and strategies to achieve it

In a nutshell your business plan can be used to obtain funding such as new loans, new investors and to obtain funds from grant makers. However, it is also your roadmap that you can refer to make sure you are headed in the right direction to meet your business goals. Within your business plan you will have outlined your operating procedures that list the steps you will take daily in running your business which eliminates guesswork and helps you train those you may hire. Your business plan will keep you focused on your business goals, costs, on track for overall growth and can be updated as needed with new ideas, financial projections and target goals.

Whether you currently have a business plan or not, if you are new to business or a seasoned vet, it's worth the time and effort to create and/or update yours. There are many resources to help you write your business plan or if you don't want to go the DIY route, you can hire someone to do it for you. When I wrote my first business plan for one of my first companies, it was an eye opener. I was able to see my business on paper, work out any kinks in the budgeting, and identify processes and strategies while also planning for the future growth of my business. If you need help writing your business plan, a simple google search for 'business plan templates' can help or you can hire an expert to do it for you.

Licenses and Certifications

Depending on your business type and industry, there are certain requirements that you need to legally run your business. For example if you want to sell a house to the public, you need a Real Estate License. If you want to work as a Cosmetologist you will need to obtain a Cosmetology License in order to legally practice. You can't practice medicine without a doctorate or perform as a lawyer without passing the state bar exam.

Whatever your business or profession, different localities have different rules and requirements so we will only cover the basics. I recommend that you check with the Small Business Association as well as your local, state and federal laws that pertain to your specific business. Visit sba.gov to search for the specific requirements, licenses and permits you will need to legally operate your business in your specific locality, state or jurisdiction as well as any federal guidelines that apply.

Two of the most common requirements that you will need is a business license and a seller's permit.

A *business license* is a permit issued by the city/local government that authorizes you to conduct business in their jurisdiction. To obtain a business license visit the website for the city or locality you plan to operate your business to apply.

A *seller's permit* is a state license that allows you to sell items either wholesale or retail and collect sales tax. Most states require a seller's permit with the exception of those states that do not have statewide sales tax. Check with your State Department of Revenue or google search "seller's permit" for your state to apply online.

Having the correct licenses and certifications to run your business will not only make it legal for you to do business but can save you the headache from potential legal troubles in case of lawsuits, consumer disputes and fines from government entities for not following set local, state or federal rules.

LLCs, Corporations, Sole Proprietorships, Partnerships

When it comes to starting your business or turning that hobby into a full-fledged legal business, you must decide how you want to legally structure your business. As a business you want to ensure your business is protected and set up in a way that best fits your business structure. The basic structures commonly used in the US are: LLC, Non-Profit which is a form of a Corporation, S Corporations, C Corporations, Sole Proprietorship and Partnership. Let's look at the differences and benefits of each.*

Disclaimer: I am not a legal or tax expert. This information is not intended as a substitute for doing your due diligence and hiring or obtaining the help of certified and licensed tax/legal experts/professionals.

Sole Proprietorship – A sole proprietorship is a business that is owned and run by one person. This structure is most common for first time business owners. In this type of business, there is no legal distinction between the owner and the business entity. The downside to this is that you are liable and responsible for any debts the business incurs. The benefit is a sole proprietorship is easy to form and the owner enjoys all profits from the business

Partnership – A partnership is a legal business that is owned and managed by two or more parties who share its profits and liabilities. The benefit in this business is parties usually share costs and responsibilities. The downside to this is that like a sole proprietorship the business is not separate from the owners for liability purposes, unless the partner is an LLC.

Corporation – A corporation is a legal business entity that has the same rights as individuals. Some types of corporations include LLC, Non-profit, S Corp, C corp. The difference between an S Corp and a C Corp is that C Corp has double taxation. Most small corporations are S Corps while major firms are usually C Corps.

LLC - Stands for Limited Liability Corporation and offers its members (owners) protection from being personally responsible for the LLC debts and lawsuits. As an owner your personal assets cannot be taken to pay for the companies debts or in the event it is sued. This is the top benefit of forming an LLC, to protect your own personal assets.

Non-Profit – A non-profit corporation is an organization that operates for the benefit of the public. Profits made cannot be paid out to any shareholders or private individuals. A common myth is that those working in a non-profit don't get paid, which is untrue. Non-profits can be formed for religious, scientific, charitable, educational, literary, public safety or cruelty-prevention causes or purposes. Hospitals, universities, national charities, churches and foundations are all examples of non-profits. A benefit of a non-profit (many not all) is the tax exempt status they hold. However, certain conditions must be met to be exempt from paying federal income taxes. 501c3 corporations are an example of non-profits that are exempt from paying federal income taxes and can accept tax-exempt donations.

S Corp – An S Corporation is a business that elects to pass corporate income, losses, deductions and credits to their shareholders for federal tax purposes. This allows S corps to avoid double taxation on the corporate income.

C Corp – A C Corporation is a business structure where the owners or shareholders are taxed separately from the business. C corporations are also subject to corporate income tax.

Obtaining EIN

When forming your business you may need to obtain an **EIN or Employer Identification Number**. An EIN is a unique 9 digit number assigned by the IRS to business entities for purposes of identification. The IRS does not require an EIN for Sole proprietorships and single member LLC's. However, if you expect to hire employees or want to apply for business credit an EIN is necessary. You can obtain your EIN, for free, by visiting **www.irs.gov** and click "Apply for an Employer Identification Number (EIN)".

Business Banking, Credit/DNB#

Throughout the course of your business life, you will want to obtain a bank account strictly for your business, *a line of credit* with a reputable supplier/vendor, or both. Most major Banks such as Chase, Bank of America and Wells Fargo, etc. can help you with opening a *business account*. If you have an LLC or

Non-Profit, then you may need to provide your paperwork to that bank before an account can be opened.

Based upon your own and/or business credit you may be able to open a line of credit with certain suppliers, vendors and others. A great way to start building your credit is by obtaining a line of credit through Staples and other suppliers. Using your **EIN,** you can also apply for a **DNB** (Dunn & Bradstreet Number) which keeps credit files for businesses. As you build your business credit you will become eligible for more lines of credit with higher limits. Just make sure to stay on top of your invoices and pay on time.

Business Taxes

No matter how you form your business as an LLC, Corporation, Sole Proprietorship or Partnership, you are still required to keep track of your income and expenses and file taxes. Even in the case of non-profits that are tax exempt some form of reporting may still be required. Accounting and tax software like QuickBooks, Xero, Freshbooks and Zohobooks are a few that can help you in your small business. Hiring an accountant and certified tax expert is highly recommended. They will be able to ensure you submit required forms and filings for your business type and meet the deadlines for filing each year.

Trademarks, Copyrights, Patents

While the type of organization you form offers protection for your business, your works, ideas and inventions can and should be protected as well. Trademarks, Copyrights and

Patents are three ways to do just that. Let's discuss each, the different uses and how to obtain them.

Trademark – A trademark is a symbol, word or words legally registered or established by use as representing a company or product. It is a type of intellectual property consisting of a recognizable sign, design or expression which identifies products or services of a particular source from those of others. Most countries require formal registration of trademarks which offers legal protection to the owner. You may have seen the letters ™ or ® on products which signifies their trademark is registered and the mark protected. Women Entrepreneurs who have a unique name, motto, logo, slogan or symbol to represent their business may want to register it as a trademark. Visit the U.S. Patent and Trademark Office at **www.USPTO.gov** to apply. There is a fee to register a trademark.

Patent – A patent is a right granted to an inventor of a product by the federal government that excludes others from making, selling or using the invention for a set period of time. An invention can be patented if it has a useful purpose, has patentable subject matter, is novel and non-obvious. The patent could cover a composition, production process, machine, tool, new plant species, or an upgrade to an existing invention. To see if your invention meets the government guidelines, you can apply at **www.USPTO.gov** , a fee applies.

Copyright – A copyright, © is an exclusive legal right given to an originator to print, publish, perform, film, or record literary, artistic, or musical material and to authorize others to do the same. If you are an author, poet, screenwriter, songwriter, etc. you may have use for a copyright to protect your work. To obtain a copyright visit **www.copyright.gov** to register. If you have original blogs, social media posts and/or short online articles, there is a new group registration being offered at **www.copyright.gov/grtx** for you to apply.

Contracts and Business Policies

When selling certain products or services, especially those of a high end/high ticket value it is often imperative that you have a **Contract** outlining your criteria and contractual obligations. While there are many templates for contracts online for just about every type of business, product and service, it is highly recommended you have an attorney look over your contract prior to use. Some attorneys will review it for free or at a low cost and recommend any necessary changes, corrections or additions. You want to make sure that in the event of a dispute or lawsuit, you and your business is covered while customer expectations are also detailed and made clear.

For every business, there are certain policies regarding business practices that you want to outline for your customers and clients. A **Business Policy** is the guidelines you set for your organization to govern your business actions.

For those of you who are collecting personal and/or sensitive information a **Privacy Policy** is also needed. In 2020 California recently passed a privacy law that has changed the way a lot of companies are allowed to handle your personal information, giving consumers the right to request a copy of their data collected and request removal. So when creating your Privacy Policy, detail how you are keeping your clients' personal information safe. Under EU law, GDPR policy states you must obtain the informed consent of the user before subscribing them to a service. So make sure to check any state or federal laws to ensure your practices comply.

If you are selling products you may consider offering a **Return Policy**. In the event of a dissatisfied customer will you offer a cash refund policy, only allow exchanges or no refund at all. And if you do, how long will they have to get that refund or exchange? This needs to be clearly posted at the time of purchase whether online or offline. The last thing you want is for a customer or client to try to return or request a refund and you have no clear policy posted. This almost always leads to bad business, bad reviews, bad word of mouth and even lawsuits.

Another type of business policy is a **Guarantee**. You may have seen offers where companies offer *Money Back Guarantees* if their product doesn't work for you. Or there may be a *Satisfaction Guarantee* where the company may agree to return a portion of what you paid or exchange the product for another.

You also may want to consider internal policies, especially if you have employees. Think of the policies that were in place at companies you have worked for in the past. Was there an **Attendance Policy, a Confidentiality Policy, an Anti-**

Discrimination Policy or a Code of Conduct? These are all policies that govern the actions that you as a business owner will take as well as clear expectations of how you will run your business. When coming up with your own policies, it is okay to look at what is working for other businesses and adjust accordingly.

Loans, grants, funding for your biz...which way will you go?

Now let's talk money! We all know the saying that it takes money to make money. This definitely rings true for us Women Entrepreneurs who are on the road to success as we start and grow our businesses. Money, or funding can literally make or break your business. Remember from Chapter 3, one of the top Dream Killers was "No Money" and lack of funding is one of the main reasons many businesses fail or even never get started. One purpose of this **"Mind Your Business Lady"** guide is to make sure that none of my readers allow that dreaded Dream Killer of not having the money to start or grow your business stop you from achieving and receiving all that God has planned for you.

When we think of traditional ways to fund a business, the most common ways are to take out a loan (business or personal), to use your savings, to get investors or apply for grants. Each of these ways comes with their own set of pros and cons and some may be more difficult to obtain than others depending on your own personal/business credit file. The following table lists some of the pros and cons of each and how to apply. These are all traditional ways to find funding for your business.

	LOANS	SAVINGS	INVESTORS	GRANTS
P R O S	Amounts are usually enough to cover expenses	You don't have to worry about paying anyone back	Multiple Investors can cover expenses/cost	Free money you do not have to repay
	Can be easy to obtain with great credit	Easy to access, no forms, apps to fill out	Low criteria, usually not dependent on credit	Can obtain multiple grants for different projects
		Little to no waiting period	Can be obtained with a great pitch	
C O N S	Must qualify, credit, documents, etc.	You may deplete your life savings, retirement	Investors will want increased return on their investment	Not easy to locate, especially for-profit businesses
	Has interest to repay	May be penalties for withdrawing if from IRA, etc.	You may have to give away a share in your company	Have strict guidelines to qualify
	Must be repaid on time	Must be a substantial amount to	Funding may be trickled out	May have to re-apply yearly for

	LOANS	SAVINGS	INVESTORS	GRANTS
		cover all expenses		continued funding
			Investor may drop out if results aren't seen	May not be enough to cover all expenses
HOW TO APPLY	Banks, Small Business Assoc.	Submit withdrawal request	Rules vary, the key is to locate and pitch	Locate grant makers and apply

As you can see from the table above, each funding type has its own set of pros and cons. I am sure you can think of a few that are not listed yourself. The important thing to remember is to make sure you dot your i's and cross your t's when applying for funding and making sure your business is legally able to operate. Make sure you know the requirements, qualifications and have all necessary paperwork ready to submit.

Putting together a funding package with your basic documents and information will save you time, as well as keeping a log of where you are applying and the current status of all applications. Make note of any deadlines and always follow up via phone and email to the contact person to keep your lines of communication open and stay on top of any unforeseen issues.

CREATIVE FUNDING IDEAS, MAKING INVESTING IN YOURSELF & BIZ A PRIORITY

So we have covered the traditional ways you can use to obtain funding. Most business owners consider traditional funding first and often struggle and stress when it comes to getting the money to start or grow their business. If you are anything like me when I first went into business for myself as well as when I needed funds to grow my business, you may not have everything that is required to secure a traditional loan. Or you may not have a huge savings to tap into, access to investors or qualify for grants that are mostly given to non-profits. (Note: I did qualify and receive a technology grant for about $1500 years ago that did help out but in no way covered my business expenses.)

So how did I, a working Mom, living paycheck to paycheck, drowning in student loan debt, with horrible credit, no savings and no rich Uncle to invest in my business fund not one, not two, not three or four, but 5 businesses without having to rob a bank? The answer ladies is I had to get creative. I had to find ways that were out of the box, often overlooked that I could use to make money to fund my businesses.

When I look back now I smile because I truly had to brainstorm and find legal ways to fund my dreams. I call it **Creative Funding,** which we discussed a bit in Chapter 3. It is simply creative ways you can use, with little to no experience to quickly make money to fund your business. Think about it, business licenses cost, supplies cost, renting an office or building costs, business cards cost, websites costs, ads, flyers and marketing costs, creating or purchasing products costs, shipping costs, taking on more customers/clients costs and the expenses can add up quickly.

Investing in you and your business is a must and yes there is a pretty price to pay. But no worries, you got this. Where there's a will there's a way. Check out the list below of **Creative Funding Ideas** you can use to make money to fund your business and finally put that Dream Killer of "No Money" to rest. And while you're at it take out a pen and pad and brainstorm some of your own Creative Funding Ideas that you can add to the list.

CREATIVE FUNDING IDEAS

• Register with Upwork	• Babysitting
• Secret Shopping	• Garage Sales
• Focus Groups	• Offer Up/LetGo
• Recycling	• Craigslist Etc. Jobs
• Register with Fiverr	• Bake Sales
• Product Raffles	• Resume Writing
• Admin Work	• Childcare/Pick up
• Flea Markets	• Sell Your Gifts/Talents

Whew! I know after all the legalese of registering, licensing, copyrights, trademarks and patents, you still may feel a bit overwhelmed. And the idea of finding funding may have you a bit hesitant at the least. But please ladies, don't let it get you down. Start with the minimum of obtaining your business license and any sales permits you may need. Invest in your business and yourself with what you have now. Then as you "grow" along, consider your other options and obtain them as your time and funds permit.

F.Y.I. - A great resource for getting your LLC or non-profit completed in record timing is through a company called Legal Zoom. Visit **www.legalzoom.com** to get your paperwork completed and submitted to the correct government agencies for you. The most important advice I can give is don't neglect to protect your business and your business assets. Having your i's dotted and your t's crossed will benefit you well in the long run. So by all means, take a deep breath, get help if you need it and get it done.

CHAPTER 4 TAKE-AWAYS

- If you don't have a business plan, get it done.
- Are your licenses and certifications complete and up to date?
- Ensure you have the proper business structure in place to best protect your business?

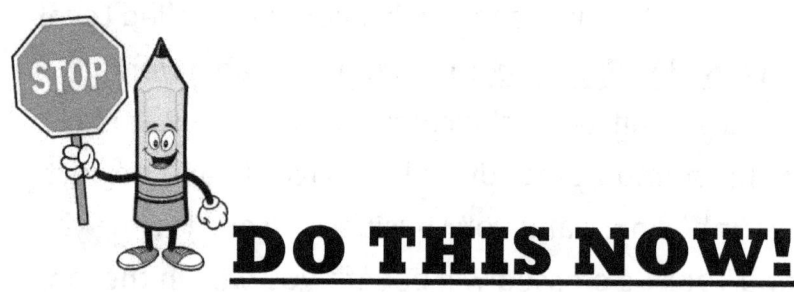

DO THIS NOW!

❖ WRITE DOWN WHICH TRADITIONAL AND/OR CREATIVE FUNDING OPTIONS YOU WILL USE TO START OR GROW YOUR BUSINESS. BEGIN A FILE OF ANY NECESSARY DOCUMENTS YOU WILL NEED FOR FUNDING/CREDIT APPROVAL.

CHAPTER 5

ONLINE VS. OFFLINE

When it comes to my Business Consulting Clients I have helped those who have storefront/brick and mortar businesses as well as those who operate strictly online. Many have a combination of both. From Boutique Owners to Salon Owners who have storefronts as well as an online presence to Coaches, Virtual Assistants, Web designers and more who do not need or want a storefront. I personally do not have a brick and mortar location for my business.

Depending on your type of business, your needs as well as those of your clients, it is necessary to choose how and where you will conduct your business. Do you need a storefront or office, where you will work in daily, hire employees and be open to the public? Or do you need a simple website where you can have your online presence as well as conduct sales via the internet? Maybe your business would benefit from having both? Knowing where you will operate, online or offline or both, and the benefits of each is a must. In order to mind your business and achieve the ultimate goal of success you must know how to navigate in both online and offline spaces.

There are many benefits of operating your business strictly online just as there are benefits to opening an office or storefront. When I started out as an entrepreneur, I was still working a 9-5 for a fortune 500 company where I had to come into the office every day. One thing I knew without a doubt, even before I knew what I would do, was where I wanted to do it. I was so frustrated in my day job and I hated being cramped in an office. I didn't like the fact that I had to be tied to that place day in and day out for most of my day. I knew whatever business I chose would allow me the freedom to work from anywhere, to create my own hours and not be tied to a building or office to do it.

I had dreams of not just working from home, but working while sipping mimosas on the beach, or lounging in a hammock by the water while on vacation. I wanted to be able to make money in my pajamas and while I slept. Dreams to not only be the boss in my own business but to be the boss of my life. To take back my time and have the freedom to live life as I pleased without having to worry about if and how my bills would get paid.

So for me it was hands down an easy choice that I would run my business online at least 90% of the time. And thankfully as an Author, Business Consultant and CEO of the Sistars Women's Empowerment Network I am able to do just that. So let's dive right into the benefits as well as the pros and cons of running your business online vs. offline. This way you can choose which best works for you and your clients.

Online Businesses

There are many perks of running your business online. The cost of starting your online business can, in most cases, be relatively low. Depending on your business type and structure you can start an online business from as little as $0 to a few hundred dollars. The tasks of a website, customer service, email marketing, advertising and social media marketing can either be done by you or outsourced for a low price using services from websites like fiverr.com and upwork.com which are two of my favorites for great work at affordable prices.

Another benefit of operating an online business is the flexibility it gives you to work wherever you want. As long as you have a laptop or even just a smartphone and a good internet connection, you are in business. You can set up in your local coffee shop, like Starbucks, hit your neighborhood library or my favorite take a working lunch at your favorite restaurant. The possibilities are endless, I even enjoy working by the water using my cell phone's hotspot as I write on my laptop enjoying the peaceful, beautiful scenery. Working at home is also an option, not having to even get out of your pj's if you don't want to. It is a running joke between many online entrepreneurs who will get dressed from the waist up to conduct online business meetings, while having pajama pants or sweats on the bottom. Girl put some pants on…or not.

In this current day and age there are over 4.39 billion people online. Over half of the population use their mobile devices to access the internet. So it is safe to say that your online business will have access to an ever growing number of potential clients to potentially see and buy your products and services. And when you add the power of social media sites like Facebook, Twitter, Instagram, LinkedIn, Periscope, Snapchat and others, you can target your efforts towards your Dream Clients and target audience with ease.

Running your business online also makes it easy to track your stats and keep accounting of your sales, customers and inventory. When clients or potential clients fill out forms or payment information this can easily be transferred to other apps and software for your records. Instead of having to keep track of paper receipts and physical inventory you can do it all digitally which saves a lot of headache and time. QuickBooks and other apps also make it easy when it comes to tax time often able to take some of the headache out of filing.

There are so many benefits to operating your business online. The ease of use, the low cost, the flexibility to work anywhere, the multitude of apps available to make your job even easier as well as the huge amount of users in the online space are just a few bonuses. However there are a few cons to all the pros we discussed earlier. Some businesses need a personal touch, a face to face interaction that you can't replicate in the online space. Yes you can use apps like Zoom to virtually meet with clients but those only work in certain scenarios. For instance, while they have online Personal Trainers, some clients will need that hands on help to get the exercises right and receive the motivation to not quit after the first set. And there is no way that you can give a great haircut or wash, press and curl online. You can show a house online but the best Real Estate agents almost always need to meet and assist their clients in person.

Even as the world become more automated and Artificial Intelligence becomes more prevalent there are just some customers who need that personal touch. They don't want to talk to a robot over the phone, they don't want to only communicate with you via email or video chat, they want and need to see you up close to receive the products and services they need. You need to not only consider your needs and that of your particular business, but first and foremost the needs of your customers and clients. Will running your business completely online work for them? Will having your business online best help and support your customers?

Offline/Storefront Businesses

Law Offices, Hair Stylists, Retail Stores, Clothing Boutiques, Restaurants, Gyms, Doctor's Offices, Spa Owners, Bakeries, etc. all operate via a physical location. Whether it is a storefront, an office building, suite in a strip mall or other brick and mortar building, there are some businesses that just have to have a space that they can receive and serve the public. You do have certain aspects of these businesses that can operate online but for the most part the services offered must be done face to face. Yes Door Dash can deliver food to my door, and I can indeed order a pair of shoes online or set an appointment to get a facial via a website but there are times when for various reasons we as consumers want to be able to visit a place of business to best meet our needs.

The benefits of having your business offline at a physical location are many. Customers are able to have access to your products and services in person. There is no guessing if the shoes will fit, if my meal is made right or if you are the right solution to my problem. You get immediate, upfront and personal service in most cases and are helped by a human being and not an automated system with limited preset responses.

Timing is of the essence. How many times did you need to purchase something that you needed right away? Being able to go and buy the product or service right away and not wait on shipping is always a plus. Especially for those last minute shoppers like me. And how many women do you know who absolutely live for a day out shopping with the girls. To some of us it's our favorite past time, right.

Creating lasting relationships up close and personal is definitely a perk of having a storefront business. There is nothing as special as creating relationships with those you serve. Many businesses in my neighborhood are also members of our community. They recognize us when we enter their establishment, we are asked about our family and always greeted with a smile. A level of trust is built and we are more likely to not only return as repeat customers but also to refer others. The rapport you build by having an offline, physical location is priceless.

Ease of access, less waiting time, valuable relationships and the overall personal touch your customers get by having a storefront just makes your customers and clients feel good. And when you make them feel good, they are more likely to become lifetime customers. But with anything good, there are some drawbacks that come along with it. Opening a storefront can be costly and the overhead of keeping your business open will continue to grow. Not only the cost to buy, rent or lease your space but also the utility bills, the insurance, improvements and taxes can and do add up. The other drawback is that you will either have to be there yourself and/or hire employees to run your business, which limits your freedom and flexibility with your time.

Can you think of any other drawbacks to having a physical location for your business? Whatever they are just make sure they don't outweigh the many benefits before you decide. And remember there are certain instances when your business requires a mixture of both online and offline presence. Perhaps you don't need a storefront but can use your neighborhood coffee shop to take in person meetings. Would that boutique make more money if customers were able to purchase online? Think about it and choose wisely, your overall business success is counting on it.

BUDGETING AND PRICING

We all know the saying, "you have to pay the cost to be the boss." This couldn't be any truer when it comes to being your own boss and choosing whether to operate online, offline or both. As an employee working for someone else, there are expenses we just don't have. We simply pay the cost to get there, maybe buy work clothes or uniforms, daily lunch, taxes out of your check and that's basically it. But when it comes to being a Woman Entrepreneur, the cost to be your own boss adds up pretty quickly. And it is crucial to budget and price not just your products and services you sell accordingly but also the cost to supply and run your business.

We know that it costs more to run a brick and mortar business than it does to operate strictly online. Yet in choosing either, we must carefully account for what is spent in running our business. You must develop an accounting system or hire someone else to do it for you. Although I highly recommend that even if you hire or outsource your accounting, that as a business owner you have firsthand knowledge of the money coming into your business as well as the money going out. God forbid you run into a shyster or scammer, so always keep your eye on the prize. To keep track of spending we want to always have a **business budget**. To keep track of money coming in and going out we want to keep records and receipts of our accounts receivable and accounts payable. This makes it easy to deduct money going out, from money coming in and figure out your overall profit.

The goal in every business is to make a profit. If your business isn't making a profit, then you are in the red (debt) and need to rethink your business model and strategies. Are you charging enough for your products and services? Does your business model make sense, is it scalable? Are you spending too much on overhead and supplies? Do you need to cut back on some expenses or find and create other revenue streams within your business by offering additional services? Do you need to tweak your products, services or marketing techniques to better serve your ideal clients? What can you do to lower costs and increase profits while still providing quality products and services?

Create a budget based on all of your current and expected business expenses. What amount of money do you need to allocate to each expense? For example, your websites, office rent, office supplies, ad costs, payroll, phone and utilities, credit cards and lines of credit, etc. You can use a budgeting app or program or simply create an excel sheet that you can personalize to meet your needs. When creating your budget you need to make sure you're not paying out more than you are bringing in. A budget will help you stay on top of your spending and you can eliminate or reduce expenses if needed.

Pricing includes the amount we charge for our products and services as well as the amount we pay for the products and supplies we need to run or business. Pricing your products and services should include researching your competitors costs, adding up the cost of making your product or rendering your services (including labor), as well as the law of supply and demand.

By researching your competitors, those who sell similar products and services you can price based on going market rates. You can research your competitors through google searches, their social media business pages and websites or calling as a potential customer to ask for a quote. This way, you can make sure you aren't pricing below market value and not too high above it either (unless you are selling premium or customized products and services, like a Mercedes Benz instead of a Honda for example). When pricing high ticket items or services, the key to success is making sure your products, services and marketing speak to that high end client in a way that leaves no guesswork in their decision to buy.

How much does it cost to make your product or render your service? For example, to price a product, calculate the costs of materials used or the wholesale price you paid and then multiply by 2.5 or 3. Consider the cost of labor, expertise and any customization that adds even more value to your product or service.

If you buy a plain t-shirt that you purchased wholesale for $8, your resell or retail price would be between $20 and $24 (8 x 2.5 = 20, 8 x 3 = 24). However if on that same t-shirt you added custom wording, graphics or designs you can charge even more. And if the quality is great, you put in a lot of time customizing and making it into a designer piece, then of course you can go after those high end customers that may pay you hundreds for that plain t-shirt you turned into a masterpiece.

One rule of economics that we have to also consider when pricing your products and services, is the law of supply and demand. More often, when there is low supply or high demand of a product, the price increases. While on the flip side, when there is high supply and low demand the price decreases. This helps you price your goods as well as tailor your offers and sales to take advantage of this law. If you know there is a shortage on t-shirts right when there is a high demand for t-shirts, you can sell your t-shirts for more. On the other hand when there is an industry overload of t-shirts you may have to lower your price to remain competitive as everyone else will be selling them at low prices as well to get rid of their inventory. Whenever the demand for a product surpasses its supply, you have an opportunity to make a lot of money.

My best advice when it comes to pricing the costs of your supplies and services is to shop around and stick to your budget. Pay attention to reviews and referrals from those you trust and know when deciding where to spend your money. Limiting what you spend on your business and pricing your products and services accordingly is one way to ensure a profit.

There are some tools that you will need to run an online business successfully that you may also need for your offline business. Below is a list and definition of each. Study them and apply them to your business as needed. Whether running your business online, offline or a mixture of both as a Woman Entrepreneur you will need to know what works for your business to help you best serve your customers/dream clients.

Website: one or more pages located on the World Wide Web and connected to the Internet. While websites are great, every business does not need one to get started. Having an online presence is recommended for all businesses but can be done via social media sites and sites like about.me or yelp.

Domain Name Registration: In order to purchase and use a unique name for your website you must register it and pay a fee to own it. Usually this fee can be paid yearly through sites like GoDaddy.com where you can also check availability of your site name.

Site Hosting: After you register your site name, it needs somewhere to live and reside on the World Wide Web. Companies that maintain servers will charge you a fee to host your website therefore making it accessible to internet users.

SEO: Short for "Search Engine Optimization", this is the process of increasing the quality and quantity of visitors to your website by increasing your site visibility on various search engines. This works by placing keywords in your website that users are most likely to search for as they relate to your business. Those with high SEO ranks are usually listed first on search sites like Google and Yahoo.

Email Marketing: Sending email communications detailing news, your offers, events etc. to those leads and clients you have collected email addresses from and obtained their permission to add to your list. Email marketing apps also make collecting and building your email list that much easier to get the word out about your products and services.

CRM: CRM stands for "Customer Relationship Management" and in a nutshell allows you to analyze data about your customers and leads, track your interactions, focusing on customer retention and driving sales growth.

Advertising: Methods you will use to market your business and gain new customers. You can advertise in print via newspapers, magazines, flyers, billboards, banners, etc. or you can advertise online through Facebook/social media ads, Google AdSense, on your website, or social media business page.

Referrals: Word of mouth and other ways your current customers tell others to try your products or services. Offering referral bonuses to current customers as well as those whose clients may need your service is a great way to grow your customer base and revenue.

Discounts/Promo Codes: Instead of offering ongoing sales, you can use codes that customers can use to get a percentage off, two for one offer or similar discount.

Social Media: All businesses need to be present on social media networks, like Facebook, Instagram, LinkedIn, Pinterest, Twitter, etc. Find where your dream clients hang out online and make your business presence known by creating a professional page and posting valuable and consistent content as well as your offers so they know how and where to buy.

Scheduler: An online app that automatically schedules appointments or bookings.

CHAPTER 5 TAKE-AWAYS

> ➢ Online businesses offer many benefits, including low cost of operation.
> ➢ Storefront/Brick & Mortar businesses still need some form of online presence.
> ➢ Creating a business budget is a must. Track your accounts payable as well as your accounts receivable. Hire a certified CPA and/or Tax Attorney as soon as possible.

DO THIS NOW!

❖ Think about your target audience. Do they spend more money offline or online? Is your business presence visible where your target audience spends their time? Do you need to be more present online, offline or both?

CHAPTER 6

ATTRACTING THE CLIENT OF YOUR DREAMS

WHAT IS A DREAM CLIENT?

Before we learn how to attract our Dream Client, we have to know what and who this person is. A Dream Client is that client that is not only the perfect person to buy our products and services but more importantly a Dream Client is that person that our products and services are perfect for and will get them the best possible results. A Dream Client isn't based on how much money they make, where they live or what they drive.

A Dream Client is the client that you dream about working with, a client who will make your job that much easier because your products or services were made just for him or her. A Dream Client is one you don't have to chase and you don't have to struggle to make the sale because the solutions you provide speaks directly to their problem. A Dream Client will seek you out. A Dream Client won't haggle over your prices because they know what you have to offer is just for them and the transformation they will get by working with you or purchasing from you is priceless.

Whether you are running a service based or product based business, we all have those Dream Clients that we would love to do business with. The first step is to identify your Dream Client, the second step is knowing where to find your Dream

Client and the third step is landing your Dream Client which includes knowing how to speak to their pain points, needs and wants as well as nurturing those clients once you do land them.

Step 1: IDENTIFYING YOUR DREAM CLIENT

Who is your Dream Client or as some call it, your ideal customer? In order to answer this question you must figure out exactly what your Dream Client wants, needs and what makes them tick. What is their pain point or their struggle? Is there a problem that they are currently dealing with that your product or service provides a solution to?

What does your Dream Client want or need? Do they want to look younger, lose weight, get healthier, dress better, start a business, learn how to do something, get better at doing something or learn how to do what you are already an expert at doing? Do they need help fixing their credit, planning a vacation or planning/hosting an event or wedding?

Do they need something customized or created especially for them such as custom clothing, business supplies or logos? Do they need the help of someone who can complete a task for them like writing a resume, being a nanny for their children, taking professional photos, ghostwriting their book, creating ads or social media marketing? Do they want to save time, money or the headache of having to do something themselves?

What makes him/her tick, how does he/she feel right now?

After you are clear on what your Dream Client wants and needs, you must find out what makes them tick? What feelings, pains and struggles is your Dream Client dealing with as a result of not having that want or need met? Is she frustrated because she has struggled with getting her business off the ground and is ready to give up? Is she in tears because she is in debt, keeps getting denied for credit and can't provide her family with the things they need because she is drowning in high payments? Does your Dream Client fear succumbing to a major health issue because she doesn't know what to do to get healthy? Is your Dream Client so busy she just doesn't have the time to plan her wedding while working and going to school? What pain is your Dream Client feeling that your product or service will resolve?

An important thing to know is the reasons behind why people buy a product or service. A quick google search will break down many reasons people buy, but they all fall under two main categories. The truth is people buy based on their emotional needs and wants, which directly relates to the two categories below. So think of these things when you are identifying your Dream Client. Also think of all the things you have purchased in the past week and which of the two categories below your own purchases fall under.

1. **People buy to avoid pain or a loss**
2. **People buy to gain pleasure**

So which category does your product or service fall under? To avoid pain or to gain pleasure? What pain or loss does your Dream Client want to avoid? What pleasure does your client wish to gain? How does your product or service help your Dream Client do either or even perhaps both? These are the questions you must answer in order to fully know and identify your Dream Client. Look at the example below from two different businesses. Business A is service based and Business B is product based.

Business A – Anytime Delivery Cleaners (Open 24/7, 365)

A Clothing Cleaner Service that is open 24 hours a day and 365 days a year and they provide pick-up and delivery service. Their Dream Clients buy their services to:

- ✓ Avoid the pain(hard work) and loss of time in washing their own clothes
- ✓ Avoid loss of time driving to the cleaners
- ✓ Avoid the loss of time looking for someone open on holidays
- ✓ Avoid the pain(stress/frustration) of not having clean clothes when they need them

Business B – Lucy's Luxury Seats (Covers, Massage Inserts & More)

Sells seat covers for cars, office and home. Multiple styles, designs, fabrics and massage inserts available. All seating is handmade, quality fabric, and one of a kind. Their Dream Clients buy their services to:

- ✓ Gain the pleasure of sitting/driving in comfort, it makes them feel good
- ✓ Gain the pleasure of having seating of the style and design to match their décor/taste
- ✓ Gain the pleasure of having something unique or different from the main stream
- ✓ Gain the pleasure of status by having high end one of a kind seating

So from the two examples above think of what pain your products/services help your Dream Client avoid or what pleasure your products/services help them gain. How does your product move your Dream Client further away from their point of pain or closer to their point of pleasure?

Step 2: LOCATING YOUR DREAM CLIENT

Locating your Dream Client is the next step in attracting the client of your dreams. This may take some research but your true Dream Client should not be hard to find. In fact, once you really get to know your Dream Client and how your product or service can solve their problem, you will get to a place in your business where your Dream Client will find you. Your Dream Client will be one of two places and for some of you, your Dream Client will be found both places, Online and Offline.

Here are some places you may *find your Dream Client*:

Online

- ✓ Social Media Networking Sites like Facebook, Instagram, LinkedIn, Twitter, Meetup, etc.
- ✓ Blog posts readers and those who comment
- ✓ Podcasts listeners
- ✓ Review and listing sites like Yelp and Yellow Pages
- ✓ Your Own Website and Other Website Community and Chat Boards
- ✓ Freelance Sites like Fiverr.com and Upwork.com
- ✓ Help them find you, put your web address, email, contact info on everything

Offline

- ✓ In person Networking Events
- ✓ Audience at Speaking Engagements
- ✓ Trade Shows
- ✓ Vending at Events
- ✓ Local Fairs and Conventions
- ✓ Your Storefront or Neighborhood Businesses
- ✓ Local Chamber of Commerce Events/Membership

When locating your Dream Client one thing you must remember is to focus on PR. Many think of Public Relations when we refer to PR. However, when I mention PR, I am referring to *building Partnerships and Relationships*. This is so important and will not just help you gain new clients but also keep the ones you have happy while also growing your business.

At the start of my Business Consulting journey, way back in 2003, I was completely unknown and had little to no clue on how to attract clients. In fact my very 1st client found me after working with me in an organization where I was volunteering my services. She saw my work skills/ethics and begged to hire me to help her grow her business. From this one client, by building an awesome work relationship with her, she referred me to another client and that client referred me to another and the ball just kept rolling. I would get a referral, do great work, make awesome connections and continue to get call after call asking to hire me. My first few years in business were all based on referrals and the relationships I built with my clients and potential clients. I spent $0 on advertising and marketing and had more clients than I could handle.

Making PR a priority in your business is the difference between locating your Dream Client versus getting stuck with a Nightmare Client. When you build partnerships with others who complement and refer your business and create lasting relationships, your business will grow in leaps and bounds. You will not only be able to locate your Dream Clients with ease but they will seek you out. Nothing I dislike more than getting an email, call or inbox message from someone I don't know trying to sell me something I don't want or need. You know the feeling, spamming has become a trend that unfortunately just causes you to be blocked or ignored. So don't do it!

Locating your Dream Client is simple. Make sure you do these 3 things:

1. **Find where they hang out**
2. **Research where they are already spending their money to make sure they're a fit**
3. **Offer valuable information where they hang out to build the like, know & trust factor**

And last but not least, research, research, research. Don't be afraid to ask questions and when possible answer their questions as it pertains to your expertise. Attracting your Dream Client is an ongoing process. Just as you and your business needs evolve over time so do those of your Dream Client.

Step 3: LANDING & NURTURING YOUR DREAM CLIENT

So you have identified and located your Dream Client. Now what? How do you land that client and close the sale. And how do you continue to nurture that client so that they will buy again and refer others to do the same? You do this by having the right Messaging that speaks to your Dream Clients' wants, needs and pain points, being bold enough and knowing what to say in Asking For The Sale & providing timely and quality Follow-up/Customer Service.

Messaging 101

Your messaging is what will speak to your Dream Client and has the power to either draw them in or run them away. The right messaging will make your Dream Client feel understood, cared for and make them want to buy from you. The wrong messaging will make them feel confused, unclear if your product/service is right for them or have them completely ignore you altogether.

Let's look at the factors that make for great messaging as you work to land your Dream Clients.

- ✓ **Sharing your personal story or your brand story**
- ✓ **Relating your product/service to their pain or problem**
- ✓ **Sharing the transformation/results & a clear step to purchase**

Here's an example of great messaging that has helped me land my Dream Clients and includes all the factor above:

"I used to play small and hide in the background. I was perfectly fine using my gifts and talents to help my employer make millions while I lived paycheck to paycheck. It wasn't until I had to smile and watch my boss get an award, a raise and a promotion all from my hard work that I had enough. She'd plagiarized my work as her own and even though she had the power to acknowledge and promote me as well, all I received was a small post it note on my computer that said, "Thanks!" I was fed up, frustrated, overworked, underpaid and so angry I was on the verge of tears.

I knew something had to change and fast. I finally realized that if I could use my God given gifts and talents to make my boss millions then I could use those same skills to succeed in my own business and equip current and aspiring Women Entrepreneurs to do the same. I took all those gifts and talents I'd been wasting in my 9-5 and turned them into money making skills and strategies to run my own business consulting and teaching other women to do the same. I went from living paycheck to paycheck to 4-figure days and 5 figure months. I went from working making my employer millions to teaching women how to make their own millions.

- → *If you are a current or aspiring Woman Entrepreneur frustrated, feeling stuck in your 9-5 or confused about how to make money in your own business*

- → *If you have tried everything, read the eBooks, listened to the gurus and webinars but still have made little to no progress or revenue*

- → *If you want the freedom to do what you love, love what you do and get paid to do it*

Then I am here to help you. As a Mother, Wife, Business Consultant, Author, and CEO of my own Women's Empowerment Organization, I know how hard it can be to juggle life, family, your j.o.b. and still run a successful business. You don't have to figure it all out on your own.

*Using my **F.A.S.T. Track To Success** method and proven success strategies my clients have:*

> *-Written & published books with little to no writing skills in 30 days or less*
>
> *-Created 6 & 7 figure businesses doing what they love without having to be tech/social media/marketing geniuses*
>
> *-Overcome the fear and confusion that holds so many back to starting, growing and scaling the business of their dreams*

*If I can do it and so many of my clients can do it, then I can teach you to do it too. Let's not waste another minute stuck and confused on what to do and how to do it. You deserve to be successful. It's time you get clear on the action steps you need to take to start or grow your business today! Schedule your free Business Clarity Call at **bit.ly/BizClarityCall** now, your future is waiting!"*

And there are so many examples of great messaging out there. Just look at the messaging of some of the products and services that you have purchased. What about the message drew you in? What pain point did you identify with? What was it that made you click the buy now button? Great messaging may take some practice and a little tweaking as you take note of what your Dream Client responds to but taking the time to get it right is so worth it. It can be long form like my example or short, sweet and straight to the point.

ASKING FOR THE SALE

Now we are at the good part of attracting your Dream Client and that is asking for the sale. It's the part where you show me the money honey. It is when a potential client or lead becomes a customer and the exchange of funds for products or services takes place. This is the part when you include your Call To Action and tell them what to do next. This is the part, where if done right will make your Dream Client, you and your bank account happy. The problem or should I rather say the fear, comes in the most here, when it is time to ask for the sale. And that fear comes in for most of my clients because they simply don't know what to say and how to say it.

You've probably heard a lot about sales scripts and sales calls. Sales scripts were often used in many of my j.o.b.'s and told you exactly what to say almost to the letter when attempting to sell to a potential customer on the sales call. The problem with Sales Scripts are that they are cookie cutter and meant to be used for every customer which doesn't always work so well.

Why? Because just like every person is different, so is every potential customer or client. This especially rings true when we are working to attract our Dream Client. No two clients are the same. Each client although similar has their own set of needs, wants, problems and pains. They think different, speak different and communicate different, which is why a basic cookie cutter sales script won't work for everyone.

So instead of focusing on Sales Scripts and Sales Calls, we are going to focus on Simple Conversations when we are asking for the sale. **Simple Conversations** are something that most people have experience with, so it makes asking for the sale a lot easier and less forced or salesy. We can have these Simple Conversations with our Dream Clients in a variety of places. The most common ways are over the phone, during a video chat, via inbox or email and my favorite, in person.

During these Simple Conversations our main focus is to:

- ✓ Ask open ended questions to learn about your Dream Client's needs, wants, problems and pains
- ✓ Find out what solutions they have already tried and why it didn't work
- ✓ Clearly explain how your product or service will help/transform i.e. the results they will get
- ✓ Answer any and all questions that will help them with their decision to purchase now
- ✓ Ask for the sale and get payment information

When you get good and comfortable doing the things above asking for the sale becomes natural. How would you like to pay for that credit or debit? Here is the link to get you started today. When would you like to get started? Or the age old 'will that be cash or charge' when having your Simple Conversations in person. Or "click here to buy now" if online.

One thing I must not neglect to mention is objections. You will have some potential clients who will have an objection or excuse as to why they can't buy your product or service.

Some objections are valid, i.e. your product or service simply isn't a fit to solve their problem. And that's okay that simply means they just may not be your Dream Client. But it doesn't mean they can't or won't refer you to someone else who is. So in this case always keep it cute and courteous and instead of asking for the sale, ask for referrals.

Other objections are just excuses or indecisiveness, i.e. I don't have the money or I have to speak with my spouse first. Yes there are some who just don't have the money, I mean they are really strapped for cash at the point and can't afford you. That is okay.

Or perhaps they are not the bread winner or really do make all buying decisions with their spouse. But most times when a potential client says they don't have the money they have it but for whatever reason choosing not to spend it with you. Or they really don't need to speak with their spouse, they just don't see the value in your product or service at that time.

Yet, if you have your messaging on point and if you know without a doubt your product or service can truly help them, then you can do one of two things.

1. Revisit the Simple Conversation at a later date to better understand and resolve their real issues
2. Place them on the mailing list, continue to build the relationship & perhaps sell to them later

Asking for the sale becomes easier the more you practice. And the more you ask for the sale, the more you will hear yes. I promise you practice makes perfect, just don't overthink it. Have those Simple Conversations and you will land your Dream Client over and over again. And if you think you absolutely need a script or if you find yourself getting off topic, just make a list of open-ended (not yes or no) questions you want to ask your potential clients and make sure to listen way more than you speak.

Nurture/Follow-up/Customer Service

Wooohooo! You asked for the sale and got a yes. What an amazing feeling, right? Now you're done, right? Well not quite. The next and last part of attracting your Dream Client is what you do after you've reeled them in to keep them. It's all a part of being able to successfully, **"Mind Your Business, Lady**!" We don't want just one time clients who buy one product or service and we never hear from them and they never here from us again. Nope, think again. We want repeat clients, who know us, like us and trust us and our businesses enough to go to us to fulfill their every need that our products and services fill.

Think about it. When you find a product you like, the business is reputable and they give you excellent service, will you be back? What about your favorite restaurant, your favorite brand of clothing or shoes, or your favorite airline, hotel or hair stylist? If you like what they are dishing out chances are you are going to keep coming back right? And you may just even tell a friend or two as well.

So goes the same for your own business when dealing with your Dream Clients. If you want them to keep coming back, to keep buying from you and to tell their family and friends to do the same, then there are a few things you must do after you've asked for and made the sale. Three things actually, Nurture them, Follow-up with them and give them the best Customer Service ever. Here's how we do that.

Nurture your Dream Client by:

- ✓ Continuing to provide valuable information, products and services
- ✓ Offering discounts, referral bonuses and other specials
- ✓ Engaging with them via Social Media & at in-person events

Follow-up with your Dream Client by:

- ✓ Sending "Thank You" emails/mailers and newsletters
- ✓ Asking them for referrals, testimonials or reviews
- ✓ Checking in with them to ensure product/service is going well
- ✓ Sending early bird offers on new products/services

Provide your Dream Client with the best Customer Service by:

- ✓ Asking them to complete Customer Satisfaction Surveys in exchange for a free gift
- ✓ Having a clear refund/exchange policy in place
- ✓ Offering a limited time money-back guarantee

There you have it, the 3 steps you need to take to attract your Dream Client and have them coming back for more. *Identify your Dream Client, Locate Your Dream Client and Land and Nurture your Dream Client.* Use the guidelines in this chapter to consistently attract the clients of your dreams that will not only be the perfect fit for what you have to offer but will refer their family and friends and keep coming back for more. What other creative ways can you think of to attract your Dream Clients?

CHAPTER 6 TAKE-AWAYS

➢ Focus on the needs, wants and pains of your Dream Client.
➢ Use clear and relatable Messaging to attract your Dream Clients.
➢ Be YOU! Have Simple Conversations and ASK for the sale!

DO THIS NOW!

❖ Write down or look at your current messaging. Does it relate to what your Dream Clients are struggling with, to their needs and wants? Share it with others and get their thoughts/feedback. Adjust it until it is just right and don't forget to include your Call-To-Action/Ask For The Sale.

CHAPTER 7

READY, SET, LAUNCH SEQUENCE

Get ready, get set and launch! Time to introduce or re-introduce your business to the world!

When most of us think about launching or re-launching a business it is easy to get overwhelmed with all of the things we think we have to do *before* we can start. We think of things like building a website, raising capital, creating social media profiles, leasing a building or hiring employees, etc. The list goes on and on. Add to that, the fact that most of us as Women Entrepreneurs are also wearing many other hats, raising children and a family, taking care of parents or others, working a 9 to 5 and perhaps going to school to further our education just to name a few. The load gets heavy and fear may also set in. But the good news is that it doesn't have to be that way. You can launch or re-launch your business by following a few simple, actionable steps that we will outline in this chapter. So get ready, get set and let's launch!

GET READY!

Most important in getting ready to launch or relaunch your business are the two Big M's, **Mindset and Messaging**. No matter what type of business you have. Notice I did not say money. I always tell my Consulting Clients to first get your mind right and the money will follow. Starting or relaunching your business is huge. As you work to grow it and scale it, Mindset is most definitely at the top of the list. So let's talk about that for a moment.

What is Mindset? **Mindset** is simply the thoughts you have surrounding your business, whether you're a seasoned vet or just getting started. What beliefs do you have about your ability to succeed? Do you believe in yourself to make things happen in your business? Do you think you are capable and worthy of success? Do you value and know your worth when it comes to your God given gifts and talents? What thoughts are living in your head that are either going to push you to achieve your business goals or hinder you from them? What negative, self-defeating thoughts do you need to eliminate that are holding you back and serving you no purpose?

"You've got to build it up!"

In one of my all-time favorite movies, "The Five Heartbeats", there is a scene where the singing group is performing together live on stage for the first time in a competition. Those running the competition have done everything possible to ensure the Five Heartbeats don't win, including not allowing Duck, played by Robert Townsend, to play piano as they'd practiced and prepared for in rehearsals. Instead they are given a "house" piano player, who doesn't know their music and is royally screwing up their performance. The crowd begins to boo as they are now all off beat and off cue. Some in the crowd even start throwing things at the group causing one of the singers, known as Choir Boy to run off stage in fear. As the booing continues and the ones who rigged the competition stand snickering and smiling, Duck has had enough. He runs over to the piano, pushes the incompetent "house" player off and takes over, gaining the attention of the audience and giving his band members a much needed boost of confidence. Their lead singer, Eddie Kane, jumps off the stage and proceeds to sing their song acapella, showing off his vocal skills and the true heart of the group. He belts out the words, "You've got to buuuuiiiillllllld it up!" as the others join in harmony singing, "A heart is a house for love...", Choir Boy returns to hit his high note and they go on to win the competition.

Now what on earth do the Five Heartbeats have to do with Mindset? First of all if you've never seen the movie, watch it, it is so good. Second, this scene has everything to do with Mindset. The group was in new and scary territory, their first live singing competition and the odds were against them. They were nervous and filled with thoughts of fear and doubt, especially when they were not allowed to perform as they had practiced. And I am sure when they were booed and had objects thrown at them, they simply wanted to quit. Which was apparent as Choir Boy literally ran off the stage. What happened here was they almost let their own fearful thoughts and the negativity of the audience get inside their heads and end their careers before it even started. But thankfully their piano player and lead singer were able to take bold action, release the negative thoughts and eventually win the competition. The act of Duck pushing the piano player away and taking over, the act of Eddie Kane jumping off the stage to sing acapella, and even Choir Boy finally coming back to the stage in time to hit his high note, all helped to build up the mindset of the group and turn a disaster into a victory.

There are many ways to build up and keep a positive Mindset to help you succeed in business. Life happens and at any given time along your entrepreneurial journey, you may need to pull yourself back from the Debby Downer Days and the Negative Nancy Nights. We all have them and it is no fun. Hopefully yours doesn't happen in the middle of a stage in front of an audience, but if it does that's okay too. You can overcome any situation in business and in life if you know how to maintain a positive mindset. The secret is in your choice to stay and sulk there when things don't go as we expect or do what you need to do to get your mind right, focus and move on.

Mindset Exercises, regularly listening to your favorite Motivational Speakers, reading uplifting books like the Bible, speaking God's Word over your life and circumstances, memorizing and repeating Daily Affirmations and of course surrounding yourself with those people and things that lift you up and encourage you are all tools to get your mind right and keep it that way. And more importantly, if you are dealing with any kind of trauma, depression or major life changing issue, do not hesitate to seek and get professional help from a licensed therapist. If you ever find yourself having more days where sadness, hopelessness, and the lack of motivation take over, please make an urgent appointment with your medical doctor and get the help you need. Knowing when to ask for help is another huge way to obtain and maintain a positive Mindset.

Here is a **Mindset Exercise** that I learned years ago and you can use to help you stay positive and succeed in business:

- Remember a time when you felt great or just amazing. Maybe you won an award, graduated, had a record breaking sales day, looked into your child's eyes for the first time, hit a particular goal or finally broke free from a bad habit. Whatever it is think about how amazing and joyful it felt.
- Now attach that memory to an action, perhaps a fist pump and yelling out "yesssss", or giving yourself a big hug, throwing your hands up with a "hallelujah", getting out of your seat and jumping for joy or doing a dance.
- Now every time you're feeling down, doubtful or just frustrated simply remember that time and actually do the action you assigned to it. Yes some folks may think you're a little coo-coo when they see you, but I promise you your mood and mindset will instantly change for the better. Take a moment to try it now. Instant feel good!

Now on to Big M number two, **Messaging**. What is messaging? Messaging is how and what you are communicating to attract your dream client. We talked about messaging a bit in the last chapter when it comes to attracting your Dream Client.

Messaging is not just what you say but also how and where you say it. Messaging can include your Personal Story of how you started your business and overcame a problem that you now solve for your clients. It can also include your Brand Story of how your products came to be and your unique journey to provide them to help your clients. Or it can be as simple as a slogan or tag line. Messaging is how you or your brand relates to your Dream Client. It ties the problem or pain points you or your products solve to the solution or results you are able to get them.

Let's look at a few awesome examples of on target messaging we see every day. These are relayed as a simple tag line. Notice the message these popular companies are sending here and how they are relating and attracting their Dream Clients.

Example #1

Nike – Just Do It!

Example #2

Subway – Eat fresh.

Example #3

Ford – Built Ford Tough

What message do you want to convey about your products or services? It is critical that your messaging be both clear and concise. You want to ensure that your messaging speaks to your target audience as well as clearly represents your brand. This may come easy to you or it may require a bit of research into what your target audience needs and wants.

For example is it important that they save time, save money, look a certain way, feel a certain way, maintain a certain status? Who is your product or service meant for and how do you speak to them in a way that they know it without a doubt? As stated before your message can be as simple as a one liner/tag line, included in your Personal/Brand Story or both.

Creating Your Personal And/Or Brand Story

The easiest and quickest way to create your **Personal Story** and/or **Brand Story** is to brainstorm what your business means to you, your life and those you are called to help? Tell your *personal story* of why you started your business and what obstacles you faced. Be honest and invite your dream clients in to get a real and up close glimpse of who you are as a person. Make it relatable and use your own voice when writing. Skip the technical terms and jargon.

Your Dream Client wants to be able to relate to you and your brand. Your **Personal Story** will let people know that you are human, what drives you to be the best at what you do and the struggles you overcame to succeed.

Your **Brand Story** will tell the journey of how your product or service came about or was created. Are there only organic ingredients in your product, is the recipe for your famous cookies passed down from generations, what is so special about your brand, product or service that makes you stand out from the competition.

There is no one set formula to create your Personal and/or Brand stories. Just make sure when you're writing that you keep it real, honest and true to who you are as a person and entrepreneur. And remember it doesn't have to be perfect, use spell check, have a trusted friend or mentor read it over and get it done. You can always tweak it or make changes if needed.

GET SET!

Building Your Team Without Breaking The Budget

As you get set to launching or relaunching your business/brand, your team has the power to make or break you. I cannot stress enough how important it is that you surround yourself with people who believe in you and your vision for your business. There is a saying that, "If you want to go fast, go alone. If you want to go far, go together." Building the right team to help run your business can be a beautiful thing as you grow and learn together. While allowing the wrong people in can ruin everything you've worked so hard for, so choose wisely.

There is a fine line we must walk when choosing those who will ultimately lead to the success of our business, our dream, our baby. As the Boss it is important you realize the buck stops with you and you are the final decision maker. You are in charge of how funding is spent, what systems to put in place and also who gets hired and fired. And we all know that with much power comes much responsibility.

As the boss you are also in charge of the work atmosphere, keeping your employees motivated and ensuring good morale while making sure the job gets done in a timely and efficient manner. Great communication amongst all involved is a must. This means setting realistic and clear expectations for your team, handling any issues as they arise and never neglecting to reward them for a job well done.

Three common questions that we must answer when it comes to building our teams are as follows:

1. Where do you find them?
2. What type of help do you need?
3. How much is this going to cost?

~Where do you find them?~

So where do you find ideal employees that are going to believe in you and work hard to make your vision for your business a reality? Here are a few places and ways you can locate and build your team without breaking the bank.

- Fiverr.com

- Upwork.com
- Indeed.com
- Friends and Family*
- College Students
- Linked In/Social Media
- Other online job boards

These are just a few places you can locate and build your dream team. Websites like Fiverr and Upwork are my favorite budget friendly places to find qualified employees on a budget. Fiverr is great for those special projects like design/logo work, editing, copywriting, marketing, flyers and more. Upwork has workers from all over the world who can do anything from replying to customer emails to answering incoming calls or whatever tasks you need to run day to day operations.

You see there is an asterisk next to friends and family. This is because you have to be really cautious with hiring those who are really close to you. You want to make sure that there is a clear distinction between the work relationship and the personal. And even if your friends and family agree to work for free, make sure you compensate them in some way with plans to put them on payroll as soon as possible.

You don't want to lose valued relationships and you don't want your business rules taken advantage of because someone close to you feels entitled or simply doesn't take your business seriously. A bonus on the other hand of adding family and friends, especially your children, to your business is the fun you'll have growing and learning together as you all work to build a legacy for generations to come.

College students who are studying in the field of expertise that you need help in are a huge benefit. You can hire college students who may need to gain experience and offer mentoring, intern opportunities, monetary salary or per project fees paid as needed. College students are usually eager to get their feet wet, knowledgeable on the latest trends and ideas and schedules flexible as they usually have set school schedules you can easily work around. You can locate available college students by visiting local community colleges, posting to online college message boards via a quick google search or asking your friends, associates and co-workers if they know someone.

Yet another tried and true way to locate those amazingly skilled team members is via Social Media especially Linked In. Linked In allows you to view more in depth profiles about your prospects and is a very business focused website. However don't discount the other popular social media sites like Facebook, Instagram and Twitter. A simple post asking for recommendations could just as well land you an employee or two worth more than their weight in gold who has been looking for an opportunity to grow. A great way to enlist help via Facebook is to make a post in a group that caters to business and entrepreneurship.

*Important: Make sure to vet, interview and qualify every team member, no matter where you may find them.

~What type of help do you need?~

Now that you've found a treasure trove of qualified individuals to add to your team, you must be clear on *what type of help you need.* Will you hire volunteers, interns, part time, full time, project based or seasonal? Are you able to barter or trade for services to fulfill a one time or ongoing position? Will you pay an hourly wage, monthly salary or commission? Will you make payments via check, direct deposit, PayPal, Venmo, Cashapp or other way? Will you use a payroll service or software program like ADP or Paychex?

Think about the needs of your business and the commitment level of the position when answering these questions. Are there other aspects you need that apply to your specific business needs? Just make sure that you are upfront and clear with any potential team members so everyone is on the same page.

~How much is this all going to cost?~

Building your team without breaking the bank is possible. Years ago I started my business with a team of volunteers and would outsource certain projects on a case by case basis. For instance I paid a designer on Fiverr $20 to design my first book cover. My artist sister created my logo. A group of trusted and talented friends and family helped me facilitate my Women's

Empowerment events. I have also bartered my consulting services for the expertise of others.

Take the steps below to build your dream team without breaking the bank. By following these easy steps you will be well on your way to **building the team of your dreams**.

1. Create a list of positions you need to fill to build your team. Mark the priority positions with a star so you know which team members you need right away.

2. Place an ad, inquiry, post, etc. using your chosen employee location methods. Make sure to be clear on the requirements and needs of the specific position.

3. Be prepared to interview and screen those who best match your needs and best fit your budget. Email is a great way to screen prospects but a video, phone or in person meeting should be used to conduct formal interviews so both parties can come to a mutual agreement and ask any questions that may arise.

LAUNCH!

Now that you are all prepared to *launch your business* to the world, it is time to set a date for your launch and choose a launch strategy. Your launch date can be any date of your choosing, but make sure that you are marketing and promoting prior to your launch date to build anticipation and ensure maximum exposure. You also want to make sure that your launch date is a time when your Dream Clients will be available to support and purchase your products or services. So keep these things in mind when choosing a launch date.

There are many **launch strategies** you can choose to introduce or re-introduce your business. You can choose any one or combination of the following:

- In-Person Event such as Grand Opening or Re-opening

- Virtual Event via Zoom, Social Media LIVE, etc.

- Email Blast with link to website/webinar

- Get Creative, launch via super creative marketing tactics like a Flash Mob

- Partner with other businesses to launch your product or service to their audience

As you finalize your launch date and strategy remember to make sure they work together to best reach as much of your target audience as possible. Make sure that you have a marketing plan that includes word-of-mouth, direct advertising, email, text, social media presence, radio, tv, podcast or other ways to get the word out about your amazing, must have products and services. Choosing a launch date at the beginning of the month or the beginning of the week works for most businesses.

However if your business is a salon, boutique or other business that is mostly frequented on weekends, then Saturday launches are the best. Whatever launch date or strategy you use make sure to give it your all, build anticipation using frequent reminders to invitees, get your team prepared and most of all HAVE FUN!

To increase revenue, buyers and referrals after your launch, always collect emails, take lots of pictures to share and tag attendees, get customer testimonials and send thank you notes/emails to those who made purchases. If you're doing an in-person event think about hiring an event planner and caterer if it is in your budget or at least enlist the help of family and friends to pull it off successfully.

Pay attention to what works and what doesn't as you launch/re-launch your business and adjust accordingly. Soon you'll be an expert at launching new products and services with an awesome team to help you along the way and your clients and bank account will thank you for it. And last but certainly not least always, always pray over your business. All things are possible with God, He wants nothing more than for you to prosper and you will succeed with a prayer and His plan!

CHAPTER 7 TAKE-AWAYS

- Give yourself enough time to prepare for and promote your next launch or re-launch.
- Enlist the help of your team and support group to get the word out.
- Choose creative launch strategies and most of all Have Fun!

DO THIS NOW!

- Write down what you will launch or re-launch next. Is it your business, a product or a service? When will you launch it and do you need to enlist help with ads, marketing, designs or other areas?

CHAPTER 8

FROM BLAH TO BOOMING,

BOOST YOUR BRAND

There will never be a time in your business when you're not working to improve and better serve your clients. Think of your business as your baby, constantly evolving and growing. And think of your clients in the same way. And as this growth and evolution occurs, we must constantly and consistently take note of what is working in our business and what needs adjustment.

At the time of publishing the **Mind Your Business Lady** book, the world is experiencing drastic changes in the way we live, work and conduct business. Many businesses have been forced into bankruptcy while others continue to open, stay open and thrive. The secret of those who have managed to stay afloat is their ability to adjust their branding and methods of operation when the old ways just are not working.

What do you do if your brick and mortar business is forced to close its doors? How do you handle a website or social media presence that your target market is just not responding to or buying? What is the big secret of longevity that brands like, Coca Cola, Mary Kay, Ford and others big names have? In this chapter we will answer these questions and more when it comes to branding and re-branding to take your business from blah to booming. As well as secrets of the trade to keep your business afloat no matter what the climate.

BRANDING

What is branding?

Branding is the face, look and feel of your business. It is your business' identity and includes your name, logo and design that speaks to who you are as a business and how others perceive you. Your branding is you showing and telling the world, this is who we are and what we stand for.

Think of some of the popular brands you see and use every day. You know that the swoosh symbol represents Nike and their slogan is Just Do It. What do you think of when you see the golden arches, or a picture of an apple, or the white bird on a blue background? We almost instantly know it is McDonald's, Apple and Twitter.

Branding is everything from the symbols and slogans to the colors we choose and how they make people feel. Certain colors are known for invoking specific feelings when we see them.

RED – excitement, passion, danger, energy, action

ORANGE – excitement, enthusiasm, warmth, vitality, happiness

YELLOW – optimism, warmth, clarity, happiness

GREEN – new beginnings, growth, nature, money

BLUE – calm, spiritual awareness, trust, dependability

PURPLE - wealth, royalty, richness, leadership, revenue

PINK – energy, cheer, soothing calm, romantic, feminine

BLACK – elegance, substance, power, authority

WHITE – cleanliness, virtue, health, simplicity

GOLD – abundance, prosperity, value, elegance, extravagance

SILVER – industrial, sleek, high-tech, modern, sophisticated

When choosing your brand colors it is far too easy to just pick your favorite colors and go with it. While this may work with some brands, it is recommended to match your brand colors with the feeling you want to invoke in your target audience. Do you want them to feel hungry, like royalty, health conscious, like a v.i.p.?

Whatever logo, brand colors, symbols or slogans you decide upon, they must be consistent across your entire brand. The same colors you use for your social media platforms should flow to your website, banners, business cards, flyers, storefront signs and any other promotional or advertising materials and campaigns. Another tip is to stick with 2 or 3 colors and 2 fonts to keep your brand/designs clear and not look too busy.

*For a more in depth break-down of branding colors and tips as it relates to your social media networking, visit

www.MindYourBusinessLady.com/SocialMediaCheatSheet to purchase and download your copy.

Brand/Personal Stories

As discussed earlier, one of the two best ways to market your brand is through stories. Telling and sharing your **Personal** Story and/or your **Brand Story** helps your target audience get to know you and your business on a relatable level. A *Personal Story* is your own story of how you started or why you started your business. It is useful when you are the face of your business, such as consulting, tv/media personality, book authors or other professional services. A *Brand Story* tells the story of your product or service and how it came to be. You may see Brand Stories on some of your favorite product labels or on their websites.

Using both types of stories in your branding, marketing and advertising efforts will best attract your target audience as it helps your know-like-trust factor. Something great happens when people feel like they know you, like what you're putting out there and are able to trust what you're saying and selling is honest and true. They are more likely to buy from you, not once, but over and over again.

Relaunch/Rebrand/Refocus

There will be times in your business when life happens and your sales, clients and impact may begin to decline or be stuck at a standstill. The companies who are able to roll with the punches and not go out of business are the ones who know if they need to and when they need to relaunch, rebrand and refocus.

Clues it may be time to **Relaunch**, **Rebrand** and **Refocus** in your business:

- ➢ Your sales and revenue have slowed or come to a standstill

- ➢ You're getting leads but not converting to customers

- ➢ You have an increase in abandoned carts on your website

- ➢ Extenuating circumstances that require you to change/adjust your business model

Relaunching your business is simply launching your business, product or service to the world and more importantly your target audience again. In a relaunch you and your target audience get to have all the fun and excitement of when you first launched your business to the world. But this time it will be so much better because now you should know what works and what doesn't. And now that you have this awesome guide for Women Entrepreneurs you're reading right now, you will know better and do better.

Rebranding usually entails a major, if not complete, overhaul to the branding of your business. Updating or changing your logos, colors, slogans, website designs and promotional material. Perhaps your brand has evolved, your website is outdated or you want to more effectively resonate with your target audience. Or maybe you want to attract an entirely different demographic than you are used to serving. For instance, the dream clients you served who were in their 20's & 30's have now grown and matured in their tastes and buying habits.

Refocus is needed when you have lost your passion, drive or clarity on the "who, what, why and how" aspects of growing your business. This happens for many reasons and happens to the best of us so don't be discouraged if this is you. It can be a mindset issue or a money management issue that needs to be zeroed in on and improved upon. The point is doing what you need to and have to in order to focus on and take action to meet your business goals.

***Mind Your Business Lady, LLC**. in partnership with **Sistars Women's Empowerment Network** offers a **5-Day Relaunch, Rebrand, Refocus Challenge** that can help you get your business back on track. Visit **http://www.Sistars.org/RRRChallenge** to enroll today.

From Blah To Booming – Tips & Secrets To Boost Your Business

No matter where you are in your business growth, we all want a business that is booming as we work to do what we love and get paid to do it. I have never met anyone, especially not any of my Consulting Clients who are satisfied with a business that is just mediocre or blah. Never ever! And I'm guessing that one of the reasons you're even reading the **Mind Your Business Lady** book is because you want your business to be booming too. Check out the tips and secrets below that are going to help you boost your business and brand.

- ✓ **Know when to hire an expert vs. doing it yourself.**

- ✓ **Research your biz/brand colors and meanings to match your target audience.**

- ✓ **K.I.S.S. - Keep It Simple Sis. When it comes to branding, website creation etc., a clear cut simple approach is best. No need for a million colors and graphics or flashy fonts. You want something that stands out and yet is memorable.**

- ✓ **Know where you can't cut corners, professional headshots, reputable payment system are a must.**

- ✓ **Know the importance of spell checking, please and thank you!**

- ✓ **Focus on PR – building Partnerships and Relationships that support your brand.**

- ✓ **Pay attention to what businesses grab your attention and get you to spend your money with them. What feeling do they invoke in you that you also want to invoke in your dream clients?**

- ✓ **Your brand is your calling card. Will people answer your call or send you to voicemail?**

Your Brand is a reflection of you and is forever evolving. Have fun and let your own unique personality shine through. Especially if you're the face of your brand, you want to show your target audience the real, authentic, fabulous YOU!

Take note of what is working and bringing you the desired results. Then simply do more of that. If you're attracting more leads and clients to your brand by placing a certain Facebook ad, then increase the amount you're spending on that ad. If your personal stories are increasing your following, share more of who you are and your why. And of course if something is just not working, tweak it or eliminate it altogether.

Pay attention to other brands that are similar to yours. Follow their Social Media pages and channels. Learn from those who are already successful in your field, but please do not copy and plagiarize. It is okay to apply what is currently working for others to your brand but never ever be a carbon copy of what another person is doing. The journey in turning your business from blah to booming will be exciting, personal and will boost your business if you stay true to who you are and the gifts God has given you.

CHAPTER 8 TAKE-AWAYS

- **Slow sales/No Sales are a clue you may need to Relaunch, Rebrand, Refocus!**
- **Relaunching your brand can give new life to your business.**
- **The right PR aka Partnerships and Relationships can boost your brand.**

 **DO THIS NOW!**

- ❖ Think about the current state of your brand. Is it time for you to breathe new life into your sales? Is there a product or service that did well in the past that you can relaunch, rebrand or refocus on to boost your brand? Do you need a new facelift for your entire business for a fresh start?

CHAPTER 9

BIZ ON A BUDGET/MULTIPLE INCOME STREAMS

Hey Lady…wooohoooo you have now reached and hopefully "worked" through to this the last chapter of the **Mind Your Business Lady Book**. Chapter 9 is sectioned into three parts; ***Building Your Business On A Budget, Tools The Experts Use & Multiple Streams Of Income***. If you're struggling with the "#1 Dream Killer – No Money" as discussed in Chapter 3, you will learn tips to build your business even if you have little to no money. You'll also get the inside scoop on the tools the experts use to grow profitable businesses and rules for adding Multiple Streams of income to increase your revenue and get you on your way to that 6 and 7 figure mark. Let's GO!

PART I: BUSINESS ON A BUDGET

When I started my very first business all I had was a dream of making a lot of money and providing a service that I knew a lot of businesses needed. I was in debt, living paycheck to paycheck and would laugh whenever I heard the word budget. Let me be honest, I was horrible with managing my money. Late fees were all too common, I was in debt up to my ears and right in the middle of filing bankruptcy. So as you can tell money was funny, yet I still wanted to start my own business. I knew that being my own boss, cutting my own check would lead to the financial freedom I needed so badly. And although I knew many business owners who had obtained loans, I just wasn't ready or qualified yet to go that route. I didn't have any rich relatives or friends who'd won the lottery that could just drop a few stacks in my lap for start-up costs. So I had to get creative and find ways to build my business on a budget. So what did I do?

1. I changed my thinking from "I don't have the money to start a business, etc." to "How can I get the money to start my business?"

2. I looked carefully at my personal spending habits. What could I cut back on? What bills were unnecessary? What recurring subscriptions was I paying for that I did not need? Was I wasting money eating out, buying the latest trends and technology? Then I just stopped and began to put the money I saved on these things into my business.

3. Next I looked at creative ways I could earn money to fund my business. I became a secret shopper, signed up for Focus Groups, started recycling, wrote resumes, did admin work on the side for family and friends, worked events for gigs I found on Craigslist and even watched kids overnight. This may seem like chump change but it really wasn't as I was earning on average an extra $500+ per week. All of which I poured into my business.

4. Last but not least I bartered for services. If I had a skill that I could trade for a service I needed, I would offer it.

Fair exchange that left both parties happy. Admin services for a free booth at an event, marketing services for free use of a facility and more. All creating win-win opportunities.

The most important thing to know if you are low on funds is to **<u>GET CREATIVE and use your God given gifts and talents</u>** to earn the money you need to grow your business. Do what you have to do now, so you can do what you want to do later. I hate shopping! But I sure did it with a smile on my face to earn money to grow my business. I hate traveling to the city, fighting rush hour traffic. But I was there faithfully when I worked my 9-5 and when I participated in Focus Groups. If you're serious about becoming your own boss and truly ready to *Mind Your Business Lady*, you will find a way to fund your business. Period.

To help you on your journey to building a business on a budget consider the "**Tools The Experts Use**" List in the next section. Check out the FREE tools and services that will help you start or grow your business without breaking the bank. And after you begin to grow your clients and revenue, you can upgrade to paid services and hiring your team.

PART II: TOOLS THE EXPERTS USE

Here is a list of tool the experts are using now to start, grow and scale their business. Many of these services I am using or have used. Some are free or offer a free trial, while others are fee-based/paid services.

Visit **www.MindYourBusinessLady.com/ExpertTools** for discounts on some of these services through our affiliate links, as well as updates and additions to this list.

Free And Paid Tools To Grow Your Business	
BeLive tv	**FREE**: web based streaming studio to add extra branding to Facebook Live Streams
Boomeranggmail	**PAID:** take control of when you send and receive email messages
Buffer	**FREE:** share to, schedule and manage your social media accounts
Canva	**FREE:** graphic design platform to create visual content, social media graphics
Cash app	**FEE BASED:** peer to peer mobile payment app
Constant Contact	**PAID**: email marketing software, FREE Trial available
Createherstock	**FREE:** Digital "pantry" of photos stock imagery
Desk.com	**PAID**: customer support engine, integrates with Salesforce

Free And Paid Tools To Grow Your Business	
Dropbox	**FREE:** cloud storage to save, share files online and sync with your devices
Etsy	**FREE/FEE BASED:** online marketplace to sell handmade or vintage goods
Facebook Creator Studio	**FREE:** manage one or more Facebook pages simultaneously
FastVid Downloader	**FREE:** Google Play app for androids to download Facebook videos
FB Ads Manager	**FREE:** tool to create and manage PAID Facebook Ads
Freelancer.com	**FREE/FEE BASED:** marketplace where employers and employees can find each other
Freepik	**FREE:** graphics for your website
GoDaddy	**PAID:** domain registration and web hosting, get your website name here
Google Adwords	**PAID:** advertising system, bid to have your ads appear in search results
Google Analytics	**FREE:** service that tracks and reports website traffic
Google Trends	**FREE:** analyzes the popularity of top search queries in Google search
Gotowebinar	**PAID:** cloud based program to create and conduct webinars
HARO (Help A Reporter Out)	**FREE:** media opportunities/share your expertise with a reporter

Free And Paid Tools To Grow Your Business	
Hellobar.com	**FREE:** design floating bar messages for your website visitors
Hootsuite	**FREE/PAID:** share to, schedule and manage your social media accounts
Kissmetrics	**PAID:** Web analytics tool that defines a clear picture of users' activities on your website
Leadpages	**PAID**: high converting landing page software, collect leads, customizable
Mailchimp	**FREE**: service for email marketing, paid upgrades also available
Market Wired now Globenewswire	**PAID:** provides news distribution and social communications solutions
Meetup.com	**FREE:** find/join/organize groups to meet people with common interests
Mykajabi.com	**PAID**: all-in-one platform to create online courses, marketing campaigns, landing pages, manage customers and design websites
Nappy.co	**FREE:** images representing people of color
PayPal	**FEE BASED:** payment system to sell online and process payments
Pexels.com	**FREE:** stock photos and video app
Pixabay	**FREE:** photos, illustrations, vector graphics, film footage and music

Free And Paid Tools To Grow Your Business	
Printful	**FREE/FEE BASED:** print on demand site for t-shirts and other products
Printify	**FREE/FEE BASED:** print on demand platform to fulfill and send your products
ProfNet	**FREE:** connects experts and journalists
PRWeb	**FREE:** the highest-rated press release service
QuickBooks	**PAID:** accounting software for small to medium sized businesses
Salesforce.com	**PAID:** #1 CRM, Customer Relationship Management software
Samcart	**PAID:** eCommerce storefront and funnel system for online selling
Shopify	**FEE BASED:** commerce platform to create and customize online stores
Shutterstock	**PAID:** buy images, videos and music for your personal and business projects
Spyfu.com	**FREE:** shows keywords that websites buy on google ads and use on search engine results
Square	**FEE BASED:** Mobile payment processing service
Squarespace	**PAID:** Website builder
Streamyard	**FREE:** Livestreaming studio in your browser. Stream to Facebook, YouTube, LinkedIn and other platforms

Free And Paid Tools To Grow Your Business	
Stripe	**FEE BASED:** Payment processing software
Survey Monkey	**FREE:** tool to create surveys for your business
Taskrabbit.com	**FREE:** matches freelance labor with local demand
Teachable	**PAID:** course creation site to host and sell your courses
Unsplash.com	**FREE:** creator driven usable images
Venmo	**FEE BASED:** Mobile payment service
Vidchops.com	**PAID**: video editing service for You-tubers and content creators
Webinar Jam	**PAID**: cloud based program to create and conduct webinars
Wix	**FREE/PAID**: website building platform
WordPress	**FREE/PAID**: website building platform
Wordstream	**FREE:** keyword tool search to find keywords your business needs to drive traffic
Zoho Mail/CRM	**FREE/PAID:** online office suite including CRM, Email and more
Zoom	**FREE:** cloud platform to host online meetings, paid upgrades available

PART III: MULTIPLE STREAMS OF INCOME

Have you ever noticed that the most successful people have their hands in a few different business endeavors? Do you know of anyone who has multiple side hustles in addition to their day job? Why do you think that is so common? The answer is because multiple streams of income means money is constantly flowing in one way or another.

The average millionaire has at least 7 streams of income, so if 1 or 2 is slow or fails, the others are still bringing in the money regardless. As Women Entrepreneurs we also need to have that "hustler" gene in our bodies. We can't put all our eggs in one basket and be left stuck looking crazy if the basket falls leaving us with nothing but egg on our face.

Growing up, everyone in my family had a side hustle. It was usually something they loved to do or were just good at. Selling Avon, fixing cars, handyman duties, ride sharing and delivery before there was Uber, selling plates, doing hair, custom creations and crafts, baking, babysitting, selling cars, making jewelry, hosting parties/events, you name it they did it. And you can too!

Here are some basic rules to creating multiple streams of income that will increase your cash flow and have you on your way to millionaire status.

Rule #1 – Start off slow with 1 or 2 incomes streams

It is going to serve you no purpose to have 10 different income streams if they are not bringing in consistent income or you're putting in half-assed effort with little results. Master 1 or 2 first before you begin adding on more. Get them running smoothly first, then on to the next.

Rule #2 – MLM Programs can be a blessing or a curse, choose wisely

If one or more of your income streams is in Multi-Level Marketing do your research on the company so you know what you're getting into. What is the time commitment, what is required of you to get paid and what are others who have experience with the company saying about the level of success, the up-line management team and payment structure? Also please, please make sure you believe 110% in the product or service being sold and that you're not just a salesperson but also a customer.

Rule #3 – Have clear/separate financial and book-keeping practices

It's easy to get confused when you have multiple payments coming into the same bank account. Will you need an entirely separate bank account for each or are there ways you can easily identify and track your incoming payments? Income streams that fall under the same business, i.e. you are selling books, working as a paid speaker, offering courses and hosting events, etc. are the exception. However if you have an online boutique, a book keeping service and a pet walking service, you may need separate accounts, licenses, permits, etc. Hiring and/or consulting a CPA or other qualified attorney or accountant is recommended.

Rule #4 – Do what you love to do, not just to make money

Too many people have had their hopes let down and their pockets emptied following the next "get-rich-quick" scheme. Don't be that person whose only motivation is chasing the money. Find what you love to do and then find ways to serve others and make money doing it.

Rule #5 – Remember most millionaires aren't born overnight

Unless you're a trust fund baby, chances are you will have to put in work to create the money you desire. And a huge percent of those who are lucky enough to hit it big in the lottery end up broke. So put in the work, don't give up and be patient in the process. Coca-cola only sold 25 bottles in their first year of business. Imagine how many bottles they sell each year now!

Rule #6 – Avoid burnout and know when to get help

When you're first starting out with 1 or 2 streams of income and you're in the start-up stage, it may be necessary to go it alone. But when those orders start pouring in and your clients begin to refer other clients, you're going to need help. Running multiple businesses means getting the help you need via other people and through automation. The question isn't if you'll need help, it's when.

Rule #7 – Have fun with it

It is true when you're doing what you love, it just doesn't feel like work. Whether you have 1 stream of income or 7 make sure it is something you love. Something that keeps you excited and fits your personality. Enjoy the experience more than the money. Carve time out to spoil yourself and your team. Have fun and **Mind Your Business Lady**!

CHAPTER 9 TAKE-AWAYS

- **You can start or grow your business on a budget. Invest in your business with what you have now.**
- **Use free and low cost tools to save on expenses.**
- **Don't put all of your eggs in a basket. Work to create multiple streams of income.**

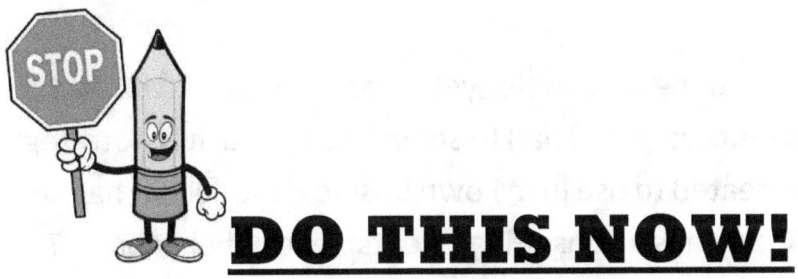

- ❖ Go to the next following 3 Bonus Sections and complete the work there. Fill out the **W.I.N. Strategy To Success**, your **Mind Your Business Lady – Custom Biz Action Plan** and checkout Bonus #3 to claim your **FREE Surprise Gift**!

MIND YOUR BUSINESS LADY – BONUS #1

W.I.N. STRATEGY TO SUCCESS

~~~~~~~~~~

There is something so simple, yet so special about the **W.I.N. Strategy To Success** that I had to share it with you. It is a strategy I originally created to use in my own business model but has also helped my Business Consulting clients reach their goals. The results are the same and spelled out in the name. If you apply and follow this strategy **you will W.I.N.** and you can use this method over and over again. It is more than a strategy for your business, but more so a strategy for your mindset.

*Visit **www.MindYourBusinessLady.com/BookDownloads** to download your free PDF fillable copy.

The strategy is outlined below, let's begin and get you on track to....

W.I.N.

W: The 5 W's of Business Success

WHO DO YOU SERVE?
_____
_____
_____

WHAT RESULTS/TRANSFORMATION DO YOU GET THEM?
_____
_____
_____
_____

WHY IS IT SO IMPORTANT THAT YOU SUCCEED?
_____
_____
_____

WHEN WILL YOU WORK ON YOUR BUSINESS?
_____
_____
_____

WHERE WILL YOU BE IN 1YR, 2YR, 5YRS IF YOU STICK TO IT? AND IF YOU DON'T?

_____
_____
_____

I: IMPLEMENT YOUR PLAN

YOU ANSWERED THE 5 W'S, NOW IT'S TIME TO IMPLEMENT. THIS IS YOUR "HOW".

WRITE OUT YOUR S.M.A.R.T. GOALS. MAKE SURE THEY ARE SPECIFIC, MEASURABLE, ATTAINABLE, REALISTIC/RELEVANT, TIMEBOUND.

_____
_____
_____
_____
_____

NOW FOR EACH GOAL ANSWER THE QUESTION, "HOW WILL I ACCOMPLISH THIS?"

_____
_____
_____
_____

WHICH GOALS CAN YOU DIY, DELEGATE TO AN ASSISTANT OR DO YOU NEED TO HIRE PROFESSIONAL HELP?

DIY:_____

_____

DELEGATE:_____

_____

HIRE PRO:_____

_____

NOW GET TO IT! DON'T OVERTHINK, DON'T PUT IT OFF FOR TOMORROW MAKE LIKE NIKE AND JUST DO IT!

N: NEVER GIVE UP

NO MATTER WHO OR WHAT, NEVER GIVE UP!

Do more of what is working and eliminate what doesn't.

Yes there will be times when people, things and circumstances try to derail you from your W.I.N. expect it. Just don't quit.

Track your results, celebrate your wins, get feedback from clients and stay focused on your goals no matter who and no matter what!

KEEP GOING SIS! NEVER GIVE UP!

TRACK YOUR RESULTS/WINS BELOW.

WIN #1 _____
_____

WIN #2 _____
_____

WIN #3 _____
_____

WIN #4 _____
_____

WIN #5 _____
_____

WIN #6 _____
_____

WIN #7 _____
_____

MIND YOUR BUSINESS LADY – BONUS #2

CUSTOM BIZ ACTION PLAN

~~~~~~~~~~

Your **Custom Biz Action Plan** is a tool I use to help clients who are struggling with the Implement part of their business. Having a clear plan of action that you can view and refer to is instrumental in you meeting your business goals. Complete the following Biz Action Plan and/or visit **www.MindYourBusinessLady.com/BookDownloads** to download your free fillable copy online.

S.M.A.R.T. Goals: Write down your goals and make sure they are Specific, Measurable, Attainable, Realistic/Relevant and Time-bound.

Implement This: What actions do you need to take to accomplish your S.M.A.R.T. Goals?

Goal Track/Wins: Track your progress and celebrate your Wins.

Support Needed: What support do you need to meet your goals and increase your Wins?

Additional Tasks To Complete: Are there additional tasks needed to accomplish and/or supplement your goals?

My Affirmations Of Success: List the positive, affirming statements you will repeat throughout your day.

***Get additional help if you need it. Remember to invest in yourself and your business and ASK for help if you need it. The success of your business is counting on you to get out of your own way and Mind Your Business Lady!

***If you're a Woman Entrepreneur who is struggling to start or grow your business, I am here to help. Schedule your free Business Clarity Call at bit.ly/BizClarityCall today. We will identify your top roadblocks to success and exactly how you can get past them. You deserve to be successful!

Mind Your Business Lady
"Custom Biz Action Plan"

NAME: _____ START DATE: _____

PROJECT/BIZ NAME: _____ DEADLINE DATE: _____

S.M.A.R.T. GOALS

- *i.e., Enroll 28 Clients Into 28 Day Challenge by next Friday Close of Business*
-
-

IMPLEMENT THIS

- *i.e., Create Lead Page and Social Media Post To Promote Challenge*
-
-

GOAL TRACK/WINS

- *i.e., 5 Enrollments after first social media post..yayyy! Ice Cream Break;-)*
-
-

SUPPORT NEEDED

- *Hire ads manager to promote on Facebook/Instagram*
-

Additional Tasks To Complete

- *i.e., Create online workbook for challenge*

-

-

My Affirmations Of Success

- *i.e., I can do ALL things through CHRIST who strengthens me! – Phillipians 4:13*

-

-

Please ensure to review your custom "Biz Action Plan" at least once a day. Your success is 100% dependent upon what you **DO**. So stay focused and keep at it. This Action Plan is meant to be used as a guide and if followed can result in you meeting and surpassing your business goals.

If you need further assistance starting or growing your business, schedule your FREE Business Clarity Call at bit.ly/BizClarityCall to day. We will identify your #1 Roadbloack to success and exactly how we can help you overcome it.

Success and best wishes from

The "Mind Your Business Lady",

Cheryle Woods

(CEO/Author/Biz Consultant)

www.MindYourBusinessLady.com

*This document as well as all content in the Mind Your Business Lady Book and/or Course are the sole property of Mind Your Business Lady, LLC and not to be shared, duplicated or altered in anyway. Any and all violations will be subject to full legal action by our legal counsel.

MIND YOUR BUSINESS LADY – BONUS #3

SURPRISE, SURPRISE

I REALLY APPRECIATE ALL WHO HAVE SUPPORTED THE MIND YOUR BUSINESS LADY AND SISTARS WOMEN'S EMPOWERMENT NETWORK FRANCHISE.

SO AS A THANK YOU AND AS A SURPRISE GIFT FOR YOU, PLEASE VISIT OUR WEBSITE AT WWW.MINDYOURBUSINESSLADY.COM/MYGIFT TO CLAIM YOUR FREE GIFT TO HELP YOU GROW YOUR BUSINESS TODAY!

IT'S TIME TO DO WHAT YOU LOVE AND GET PAID YOUR WORTH TO DO IT. IT'S TIME TO...

MIND YOUR BUSINESS LADY!

*To contact *"The Mind Your Business Lady"*, Cheryle Woods
Email: HeySistars@Sistars.org

*To enroll in any of the **Mind Your Business Lady courses visit:**
www.MindYourBusinessLady.com

***Follow us on Social Media**:

Facebook – www.facebook.com/MindYourBusinessLady

Instagram - www.instagram.com/MindYourBusinessLady

*To join our **Sistars Women's Empowerment Network** of inspiring, amazing Women Entrepreneurs visit us on social media:

Facebook Group: www.facebook.com/groups/MySistars

Facebook Page: www.facebook.com/MySistars

Instagram: www.instagram.com/sistars

INDEX

5 Daily Practices, 50, 52
5 w's, 27, 31, 145
5-Day Relaunch, Rebrand, Refocus Challenge, 126
Accounting, 2, 76, 80, 137
Accounting and tax software, 62
Advertising, 75, 85, 93, 118, 123, 124, 135
Affirmations, 50, 108, 150
Alignment
    Good things, 18
Analytics, 136
ASKING FOR THE SALE, 98
Bartering, 42
Bible verses, 22
Bible Verses
    The Parable of the Talents, 24
Biz On A Budget, 41
Biz Support System, 51
Brand Story, 110, 111, 112, 124
Branding, 122
Budget, 56, 80, 81, 83, 114, 117, 119, 131, 133
Budgeting, 38, 39, 57, 81
Building Your Team, 112
Business account, 61
Business Clarity Call, 97
Business license, 58, 71
BUSINESS ON A BUDGET, 131
Business plan, 34, 55, 56, 57
Business Policy, 64
Business Taxes, 62
C Corporation, 61
Competitors, 81
Contracts, 64
Corporation, 60
Creative, 21, 36, 37, 40, 44, 69, 103, 118, 132
Creative Funding sources, 40
Credit, 20, 38, 39, 42, 61, 62, 66, 67, 69, 81, 88, 89, 99
CRM
    Customer Relationship Management, 85, 137, 138

Custom Biz Action Plan, 149
Customer Service, 94, 102
Discounts/Promo Codes, 85
Distractions
    Dealing with..., 47, 48
Do what you love, 9, 28, 96, 153
Domain, 135
Domain Name Registration, 84
Dream Client, 87, 88, 89, 90, 91, 92, 93, 94, 95, 97, 98, 99, 100, 101, 102, 103, 109, 111
Dream Killer, 34, 37, 39, 42, 44, 46, 66, 70, 131
Dunn & Bradstreet Number, 62
EIN, 61, 62
Email marketing, 75, 84, 134, 136
Employees, 61, 65, 73, 79, 105, 113, 114, 135
Fear, 8, 17, 23, 26, 33, 34, 45, 46, 89, 97, 98, 105, 107
Friends and family, 114, 116
Funding, 18, 37, 39 40, 56, 66, 67, 68, 69, 70, 71, 113
God given gifts and talents, 6, 9, 10, 14, 17, 18, 19, 21, 22, 24, 26, 29, 30, 41, 43, 49, 96, 106, 133
Grants, 37, 56, 66, 67, 69
Grow my business, 34, 69, 133
Guarantee, 65
Identifying your dream client, 88
Invest, 11, 29, 39, 40, 44, 69, 150
Investors, 29, 56, 66, 69
IRS, 61
Journaling, 50
Keyword tool search, 138
Landing page, 136
Launch strategies, 118
Launch your business, 105, 117, 119
Licenses and Certifications, 57
Limited Liability Corporation, 60
Livestreaming, 137
LLC, 9, 59, 60, 61, 62, 71, 126
Loans, 66
Love to do, 4, 22, 87, 141

Marketing, 70, 81, 82, 84, 88, 93, 97, 114, 117, 118, 124, 133, 136
Messaging, 95, 97, 100, 109, 110, 111
Mindset, 33, 52, 105, 106, 107, 108, 109
MLM Programs, 140
Money, 28, 29, 37, 39, 42, 44, 46, 65, 66, 70, 131
Money habits, 38
Multiple streams of income, 139
Naysayers and doubters
  Dealing with..., 47, 48
Networking, 51, 92
No time, 34
Non-profit, 60, 71
Non-supporters
  Dealing with..., 47, 49
Nurture/Follow-up/Customer Service, 101
Offline/Storefront Businesses, 77
Online Businesses, 75
Online presence, 73, 84
Online stores, 137
Partnership, 59, 126
Partnerships and Relationships Building.., 92, 128
Payment processing, 137
Payments, 40, 89, 116, 136, 140
Personal Story, 110, 111, 124
Photos, 36, 88, 136
Prayer, 50
Press release, 137
Pricing, 81
Print on demand, 137
Privacy Policy, 64
Purpose, 3, 4, 9, 10, 12, 18, 19, 20, 21, 22, 29, 31, 63, 106, 139
Referrals, 85
Resources, 11, 12, 15, 20, 37, 39, 40, 42, 57

Return Policy, 65
S Corporation, 61
S.M.A.R.T. Goals, 49, 150
Saving, 38, 39
Savings, 66, 67, 69
Scheduler, 85
Seller's permit, 58
SEO, 84
Simple Conversations
  Vs. Sales Scripts, 98, 99, 101
Sistars Women's Empowerment Network, 3, 5, 9, 52, 74, 126, 153
Site Hosting, 84
Situational Stagnation, 42
Skills, 44, 46
Social Media, 85, 92, 102, 114, 115, 118
Social media cheat sheet, 124
Sole proprietorship, 59
Storefront, 73, 77, 78, 79, 123, 137
Struggle in your business, 16, 53, 72, 143
Successful business, 10, 18, 26, 27, 32, 52, 96
SURPRISE GIFT, 153
Surveys, 138
Target audience, 16, 76, 111, 118, 123, 124, 125, 126, 127, 130
Tips and secrets, 127
Tools The Experts Use, 131, 133
Trademarks, Copyrights and Patents, 63
W.I.N. Strategy To Success, 144
Website, 83, 92, 137
Website building platform, 138
Women Entrepreneurs, 1, 3, 9, 12, 29, 34, 47, 52, 55, 63, 66, 96, 105, 125, 139
Your story, 8, 16, 72, 86, 130
You-tubers, 138